THE BOOK OF ISAIAH
Thoughts as High as Heaven

Other Books by Roy E. Gane

The Sanctuary and Salvation

Who's Afraid of the Judgment?

THE BOOK OF ISAIAH
Thoughts as High as Heaven

Roy E. Gane

Pacific Press®
Publishing Association
Nampa, Idaho | www.pacificpress.com

Cover design and resources from Lars Justinen

The author assumes full responsibility for the accuracy of all facts and quotations as cited in this book.

Additional copies of this book are available for purchase by calling toll-free 1-800-765-6955 or by visiting adventistbookcenter.com.

Library of Congress Cataloging-in-Publication Data

Names: Gane, Roy E., 1955- author.
Title: The book of Isaiah : thoughts as high as heaven / Roy E. Gane.
Description: Nampa, Idaho : Pacific Press Publishing Association, [2020] |
    Summary: "The Book of Isaiah is a review of the major themes of the book
    of Isaiah"— Provided by publisher.
Identifiers: LCCN 2020024400 | ISBN 9780816366583 (paperback) |
    ISBN 9780816366590 (ebook)
Subjects: LCSH: Bible. Isaiah—Criticism, interpretation, etc.
Classification: LCC BS1515.52 .G36 2020 | DDC 224/.106—dc23
LC record available at https://lccn.loc.gov/2020024400

July 2020

Contents

Introduction

People naturally look around for ways to survive and thrive. They look to their families, friends, and organizations, and they strive to acquire lands, buildings, and material possessions for security and prosperity. Food, comfort, and safety are high priorities. When hardships or dangers arise, we look around for solutions. But what if we cannot find answers to the problems that threaten our existence?

The book of Isaiah challenges people, including us, to stop just looking *around* and start looking *up* to the Lord, whom Isaiah saw "sitting upon a throne, high and lifted up" (Isaiah 6:1). The Lord is the Creator, with sovereign power over the world and knowledge of the future (Isaiah 40–45), but He is not too high and mighty to hear and care about the least of His children. Yes, He dwells "in the high and holy place," but "also with him who is of a contrite and lowly spirit, to revive the spirit of the lowly" (Isaiah 57:15).

So "seek the LORD while he may be found; call upon him while he is near" (Isaiah 55:6).

Do not be afraid to come to the Lord because your behavior has offended Him; He is ready to generously and compassionately pardon you (verse 7). How can that be when He is so holy that magnificent, sinless seraphim veil their faces in His presence (Isaiah 6:2)? We have difficulty forgiving ourselves and other people around us, so it is hard to understand why He would forgive us. The wonderful answer is that God is not only unlike us in power and perfection but also unlike us in mercy:

"For my thoughts are not your thoughts,
    neither are your ways my ways, declares the LORD.
For as the heavens are higher than the earth,
    so are my ways higher than your ways
    and my thoughts than your thoughts" (Isaiah 55:8, 9).

Look up to His thoughts!

God can lift us up because His Servant, the Messiah, came way down to be vulnerable like a "young plant," to be "despised and rejected by men," and to bear "our griefs" and carry "our sorrows." But by allowing Himself to be "pierced for our transgressions" and "cut off out of the land of the living" (Isaiah 53:2–5, 8), "he shall be high and lifted up, and shall be exalted" (Isaiah 52:13; compare Philippians 2:5–11). Look up to the Messiah, the Christ!

To look up to a power and a love that is far greater than our own is to trust. In the first part of the book of Isaiah, King Ahaz refused to trust the Lord when he was threatened by the alliance of northern Israel with Syria—a problem too big for him to solve on his own (Isaiah 7). Rather than looking up, even when God offered to give him a sign that would be as "deep as Sheol or high as heaven" (verse 11), he looked around and bribed the king of Assyria to intervene on his behalf (2 Kings 16:7–9), with disastrous consequences.

Later in the book, Ahaz's son Hezekiah was faced with the more deadly threat of conquest by the Assyrian superpower. But he looked up, praying to the "LORD of hosts, God of Israel, enthroned above the cherubim" who "made heaven and earth" (Isaiah 37:16), and the Lord delivered him, Jerusalem, and his nation of Judah through a spectacular miracle (verse 36).

In the book of Isaiah, God's lofty thoughts and reflections about Him are expressed in some of the most exalted language in all of human literature. Much of the book is poetry that includes parallelism, vivid imagery, dramatic contrasts, and rhythm that sounds musical. There is a complex interweaving of themes in an ongoing process of elaboration and development, as in a symphony.

The first part of the book of Isaiah, consisting of chapters 1–39, focuses on judgment; the second part, in chapters 40–66, emphasizes comfort and restoration after the Babylonian exile. These themes are contrasting, but they are also complementary, as shown by significant elements of comfort in the first part and judgment in the second part.

While most scholars agree on the two overall parts of Isaiah, they have suggested a variety of literary structures to account for the relationships between the subsections of these parts. Here is one possibility, in which sections of the book can be arranged in a chiasm (here an arch structure with an isolated center of F) that focuses on the need for trust in the Lord:[1]

A Judgment and Restoration of God's People (chapters 1–6)
  B Promise of a Divine, Royal Messiah (7–12)
    C Judgment on the Nations, Including Babylon (13–23)
      D God as Conqueror (24–27)
        E Woes on People Who Do Not Trust and Obey God (28–35)
          F Necessity of Trust in God (36–39)
        E' Comfort for God's People Who Trust Him (40–42)
      D' God as Creator (43–45)
    C' Judgment Focused on Babylon (46–48)

B' Promise of Suffering Servant-Messiah (49–55)
A' Judgment and Restoration of God's People, Including Faithful Foreigners (56–66)

The present small volume is a fresh exposition of some selected portions of the final canonical form of Isaiah for contemporary readers. It is designed to illuminate key aspects of God's character and His way of leading faulty people, encouraging us to look up to Him.[2]

This book uses the English Standard Version (ESV) as the default English translation for quotations of Scripture, referring to others by their abbreviations (KJV, NIV, NKJV, NJPS, NET). As a teacher and researcher of biblical languages and literature, the author derives his interpretations from the study of the original Hebrew, Aramaic, and Greek texts that constitute the Bible. His choice of a translation does not indicate an unqualified endorsement of any English version because every translation in any language is a form of commentary produced through scholarly interpretation.

---

1. This suggested structure builds on and revises the chiasm proposed by Richard M. Davidson, "The Messianic Hope in Isaiah 7:14 and the Volume of Immanuel (Isaiah 7–12)," in *"For You Have Strengthened Me": Biblical and Theological Studies in Honor of Gerhard Pfandl in Celebration of His Sixty-Fifth Birthday*, ed. Martin Pröbstle, Gerald A. Klingbeil, and Martin Klingbeil (St. Peter am Hart, Austria: Seminar Schloss Bogenhofen, 2007), 95. A *chiasm* is a pattern in which elements are repeated in reverse order, such as A B B A or A B B' A' (with ' representing a somewhat altered repetition) or in an "arch" introversion pattern with an isolated center, such as A B C B' A'.

2. It is not anything close to a comprehensive commentary, such as the excellent work of John N. Oswalt in the two volumes of *The Book of Isaiah*, New International Commentary on the Old Testament (Grand Rapids, MI: Eerdmans, 1986, 1998). The author is currently preparing a commentary on Isaiah, coauthored with Wann Fanwar and Jerome Skinner, for the new Seventh-day Adventist International Bible Commentary series.

One

Who Do You Want to Be?

Isaiah 1, 2, 5

How much is your identity worth? It is worth enough for someone to want to steal it. Nicole McCabe, an Australian woman, was six months pregnant and living in Israel. One day she was listening to the news on the radio and heard that three Australians had been linked to a hit squad that was responsible for murdering a prominent man. One of the three who were wanted for murder was Nicole McCabe! Thieves had stolen her identity data, along with that of two other Australians, and had used her personal information to make a fake passport. Fortunately for her, she still possessed her real passport with her picture in it. The fake passport had the photo of one of the thieves.[1]

Giving up identity

Identity thieves cause significant financial harm. The consumer credit reporting company Experian has released statistics showing that 40 percent of online consumers around the world have been targets of identity theft at least once.[2] Millions are victims each year, and they lose billions of dollars as a result.

These victims have been robbed or deceived. They would not release their identity data if they knew the results. But long before telephones, credit cards, and the internet, God's Israelite people gave up their identity, not just their data, by deceiving themselves. The Lord lamented through His prophet Isaiah:

"The ox knows its owner,
    and the donkey its master's crib,
but Israel does not know,
    my people do not understand" (Isaiah 1:3).

The Israelites belonged to the Lord because they had contracted a covenant relationship with Him (Exodus 24). But Isaiah reported, "They have forsaken the LORD, they have despised the Holy One of Israel, they are utterly estranged" (Isaiah 1:4).

How much was their identity worth before they gave it up? After God gave their ancestors an identity as a free people by delivering them from slavery, He had promised them: "Now therefore, if you will indeed obey my voice and keep my covenant, you shall be my treasured possession among all peoples, for all the earth is mine; and you shall be to me a kingdom of priests and a holy nation" (Exodus 19:5, 6). Loyal Israelites who belonged to the Sovereign of all the earth as His chosen, treasured possession would enjoy wonderful benefits and privileges, including His presence among them, prosperity, protection from enemies, and preeminence among the nations (Leviticus 26:3–13; Deuteronomy 28:1–14).

Lest anyone suppose that God's promises were empty rhetoric, consider the early reign of Solomon, who "excelled all the kings of the earth in riches and in wisdom" (1 Kings 10:23; see also verses 21, 27). When the queen of Sheba came and witnessed Solomon's God-given wisdom and wealth, "there was no more breath in her" (verse 5), and she praised the Lord (verse 9).

Sadly, that was one brief shining moment in the long history of Israel. It should have continued, with God's people rising to ever greater heights for His glory, to fulfill His promise to Abraham that in his offspring all the nations of the earth would be blessed (Genesis 22:18; Genesis 12:3). But the Israelites threw away their identity and suffered the consequences of disloyalty, which Moses laid out in a series of conditional covenant curses that went from bad to worse to horrific (Leviticus 26:14–39; Deuteronomy 28:15–68). The Lord could not bless His people if they ignored His wise principles and rebelled against Him because it would send the message that He and His principles did not matter.

Centuries after Solomon, Isaiah lived in the country of Judah, the remaining southern part of what had been Solomon's empire. Judah was badly injured, so Isaiah portrayed it as full of raw wounds, bruises, and sores (Isaiah 1:6). He went on to describe the disastrous situation resulting from an invasion by foreigners, which occurred during his ministry:[3]

> Your country lies desolate;
>   your cities are burned with fire;
> in your very presence
>   foreigners devour your land;
>   it is desolate, as overthrown by foreigners. . . .
> If the LORD of hosts
>   had not left us a few survivors,
> we should have been like Sodom,
>   and become like Gomorrah (verses 7, 9).

Why would anyone choose to give up the identity with the Lord that the Israelites had enjoyed earlier in their history? That is the question to which God demanded an answer: "Why will you still be struck down? Why will you continue to rebel?" (verse 5).

The Israelites did not have an answer because there is never any sensible reason to rebel against God. Such rebellion is sin, and sin is inherently irrational. To say it more plainly, *sin is stupid*! Sin pretends to have the good reason of serving one's own interests, but selfishness violates God's principles of unselfish love. And selfishness is self-defeating because everyone's well-being is intertwined with that of others, so everyone gets hurt by selfishness in the long run.

There was more to the analogy of Sodom and Gomorrah than the pitiful state of Judah. Isaiah turned on his people and blasted them with full force:

> Hear the word of the LORD,
>   you rulers of Sodom!
> Give ear to the teaching of our God,
>   you people of Gomorrah! (verse 10).

The Judahites, especially their rulers, shared the characters of the people of Sodom and Gomorrah and deserved their fate of utter destruction (compare Genesis 19). The Bible does not report that the people of Judah in the time of Isaiah attempted a homosexual gang rape, as the Sodomites had done (Genesis 19:4–11; compare Judges 19, which tells of the actual gang rape of a woman by Israelites). But Judah's guilt was like that of Sodom; it "had pride, excess of food, and prosperous ease, but did not aid the poor and needy" (Ezekiel 16:49).

The people of Judah were not irreligious, yet God rejected their many formal religious exercises in spite of the fact that He had originally commanded them (Isaiah 1:11–14; compare especially Leviticus 1–17, 23; Numbers 28; 29). There was nothing wrong with such worship activities themselves, but the people were hypocritical rather than worshiping the Lord "in spirit and truth" (John 4:24). Isaiah did not oppose the sacrificial system itself but the abuse of it, as shown by the fact that he also conveyed God's rejection of the prayers of the Judahites:[4]

"When you spread out your hands,
   I will hide my eyes from you;
even though you make many prayers,
   I will not listen;
   your hands are full of blood" (Isaiah 1:15).

Lifting one's hands and spreading them out toward the Deity in heaven was a common way to pray in ancient times (1 Kings 8:22; compare 1 Timothy 2:8). But this gesture by the people of Judah was offensive to God because they had blood on their hands—not the literal blood of animals that they were sacrificing but the metaphorical bloodguilt of their fellow citizens, whom they were oppressing (Isaiah 1:15–17). Jerusalem was full of social injustice, including murder, theft, bribery, and failing to help vulnerable and exploited orphans and widows (verses 21–23). All of this was in blatant violation of common decency and divine law (for example, Exodus 22:22–24 [Hebrew verses 21–23]).

The way we treat God's children, especially those whom Jesus called "the least of these my brothers" (Matthew 25:40; compare verse 45), is the way we treat Him. The Lord takes this personally and judges accordingly.

God hates religious hypocrisy, which attempts to maintain a false assurance of a right relationship with Him while covering up one's disobedience to Him in other areas of life. An appearance of reverence and devotion in church on Sabbath, with generous offerings and active participation or even leadership, looks good in the community. These good behaviors are a small price to pay for a smoke screen to hide the profits of selfish ambition and the exploitive gratification of lust. But such a cover-up is futile because the Lord sees and hears everything (Psalm 139).

"To obey is better than sacrifice" (1 Samuel 15:22) because obedience to God is the primary indicator of true loyalty to

Him, which is expressed in corresponding worship. Worship without loyal obedience expresses a lie about one's relationship with God and thereby misrepresents His character. It is impossible to keep the first great commandment ("You shall love the Lord your God" [Deuteronomy 6:5; Matthew 22:37]) through worship activities while violating the second great commandment ("You shall love your neighbor as yourself" [Leviticus 19:18; Matthew 22:39]).

Consider your options!

Michael A. Cicconetti was a municipal court judge in Painesville, Ohio. Beginning in the mid-1990s, he administered what he called "creative justice" by giving a defendant a choice between jail time and an unusual punishment that fit the crime. For example, twenty-five-year-old Ohio housewife Michelle Murray had abandoned thirty-five kittens in a forest during the winter. So Cicconetti offered her a reduced prison sentence if she would spend a night in the woods.[5]

God offers options too. Isaiah 1:2–20 is a covenant lawsuit in which the Lord as the Sovereign and superior covenant Partner—and therefore, the Judge—arraigns His people on the charge of breaking their treaty with Him. They are guilty without excuse and are at His mercy. He would be fully justified if He simply annihilated them, just as He had Sodom and Gomorrah. But instead of issuing a verdict of terminal doom, or even a creative choice between two kinds of punishment, He gives them another chance to escape punishment altogether:

"Come now, let us reason together, says the Lord:
though your sins are like scarlet,
    they shall be as white as snow;
though they are red like crimson,
    they shall become like wool" (verse 18).

In this context, the Hebrew word translated as "reason together" refers to presenting or arguing a case in a lawsuit (compare Job 23:7).[6] God invites the previously unreasoning and unreasonable Judahites to join Him in a legal dialogue to weigh their options: "Come, let's consider your options" (Isaiah 1:18, NET). They need to participate because the choice is theirs.

But there would be no options without the Lord's amazing divine mercy up front: He promises to completely wipe out their guilt so that they can have a new beginning. What sense does this make? It sounds like an irrational remedy to irrational sin. Max Lucado writes,

> I've never been surprised by God's judgment, but I'm still stunned by his grace.
>
> God's judgment has never been a problem for me. In fact, it's always seemed right. Lightning bolts on Sodom. Fire on Gomorrah. *Good job, God.* Egyptians swallowed in the Red Sea. *They had it coming.* Forty years of wandering to loosen the stiff necks of the Israelites? *Would've done it myself.* Ananias and Sapphira? *You bet.*
>
> Discipline is easy for me to swallow. Logical to assimilate. Manageable and appropriate.
>
> But God's grace? Anything but.[7]

Divine love does not follow human logic. God's love has its own kind of logic.

God's people have the opportunity to choose one of two ways to go:

> "If you are willing and obedient,
>   you shall eat the good of the land;
> but if you refuse and rebel,
>   you shall be eaten by the sword" (verses 19, 20).

Eat or be eaten—that is, live or die. These contrasting destinies represent all the covenant blessings versus the curses.

The Judahites would not earn their salvation by their obedience. They would be saved already by God's forgiveness. The question was whether they would then choose to live as saved people, as Jesus told a woman whom He rescued from being stoned for adultery: "Neither do I condemn you; go, and from now on sin no more" (John 8:11). The Lord takes people where they are, but He does not leave them where they were. He saves sinners *from* their sins (see Matthew 1:21), not *in* their sins.

Like God's offer in Isaiah 1:18–20, His new covenant is based on forgiveness (Jeremiah 31:34). If a sinner truly receives and continues to cherish His forgiveness, the result is loyal obedience to Him, facilitated by the miraculous writing of His law on the heart (verse 33). The Lord's forgiveness transforms the sinner's heart not only by inspiring gratitude but also by the creative act of making a new, clean heart (Psalm 51:10 [Hebrew verse 12]). "God's forgiveness is not merely a judicial act by which He sets us free from condemnation. It is not only forgiveness *for* sin, but reclaiming *from* sin. It is the outflow of redeeming love that transforms the heart."[8]

The uniqueness of God's forgiveness, which only He can give, is shown by the Hebrew word *salakh,* "forgive"—He alone is the subject who performs this action (for example, Numbers 14:20; Isaiah 55:7).

Similarly, the Lord alone can *bara',* "create" (Genesis 1:1, 21, 27), so only He can create a clean heart, and He alone can pour love into the heart by His Holy Spirit (see Romans 5:5). This love brings the recipient into harmony with the God who is love and with His law, which is based on love (1 John 4:8, 16; Matthew 22:37–40). Those who do not allow God to write His law on their hearts receive another kind of writing: handwriting on the wall with a message of doom (Daniel 5).

United Nations at the Lord's temple mount

Following the vivid options of eating or being eaten (Isaiah 1:19, 20), the book of Isaiah reinforces the importance of choosing wisely by presenting the contrasting destinies in various ways. The oscillation between conditional promises of hope and warnings of doom gives the book a texture of alternating light and darkness. For example, "Zion shall be redeemed by justice, and those in her who repent, by righteousness. But rebels and sinners shall be broken together" (verses 27, 28).

Two of Isaiah's most striking representations of hope and doom are found in the form of a mountain (Isaiah 2) and a vineyard (Isaiah 5). The mountain is the temple mount in Jerusalem. Isaiah 2:2–4, paralleled almost word for word by the contemporary prophecy of Micah 4:1–3, is a soaring vision of hope for the Lord's future international leadership from His temple in Jerusalem.

The mountain on which the temple built by Solomon was located is not the highest mountain in physical terms, even in the immediate vicinity; The Mount of Olives and Mount Scopus are higher. But in time ("the latter days" [Isaiah 2:2]), it could have become the highest in metaphorical terms as the preeminent source of guidance for the nations, as they would recognize the supreme value of the wise instructions given by the Deity in residence there. The Lord's temple could have become the United Nations—the shrine and headquarters of peace. Wars could have ceased.

A wall outside the modern United Nations complex in New York bears this inscription, quoting from Isaiah 2:4:

THEY SHALL BEAT THEIR SWORDS INTO PLOWSHARES. AND THEIR SPEARS INTO PRUNING HOOKS: NATION SHALL NOT LIFT UP SWORD AGAINST NATION, NEITHER SHALL THEY LEARN WAR ANY MORE.

ISAIAH

The United Nations complex in New York was completed in 1952. Unfortunately, Isaiah's vision of peace has not been realized since then. Many thousands of people have died, and countless others have suffered in wars around the world, with no sign of full peace on the horizon.

What is the matter? Isaiah provides the answer: peace can come only if all nations learn the Lord's ways and walk in His paths (see verse 3). But first, God's people must lead the way to show the value of His instructions.

After revealing God's vision for all nations as a result of Judah's obedience, Isaiah 2:5 backs up in typical Hebrew effect-to-cause reasoning (rather than our modern cause-to-effect approach) to show what must happen before that: "O house of Jacob, come, let us walk in the light of the LORD." If other peoples will do this walk and have such wonderful benefits, why don't we start doing it now to enjoy the restoration that God offers? The world is dark, but His flashlight is big and bright, and in His light, we can clearly see where we are going.

Vineyard song turned sour

How much should God do for faithless people before He lets them go? Isaiah addresses this question in his "Song of the Vineyard" (Isaiah 5:1, 2, NIV). The poem tells of a landowner who planted a vineyard in an ideal location and did everything he could to make it successful. Then he looked forward to a fine harvest of edible grapes, but surprisingly, the vineyard produced worthless wild, sour grapes. It turns out that the owner of the vineyard represents the Lord, and this brief story is an illustration for the nation of Judah:

> And now, O inhabitants of Jerusalem
>   and men of Judah,
>   judge between me and my vineyard.
>   What more was there to do for my vineyard,

that I have not done in it?
When I looked for it to yield grapes,
    why did it yield wild grapes? (verses 3, 4).

The song is a juridical parable. Such a parable draws the listeners into a realistic story about a violation of a law, calls on them to make a judgment, and then reveals that they are judging themselves (for example, 2 Samuel 12:1–11; Matthew 21:33–40). Isaiah 5 does not record the Judahites' answers to God's questions regarding His vineyard (verses 3, 4). The answers are obvious: there was nothing more that He could have done, and there was no reason why the vineyard should have yielded wild grapes. So He would be justified in condemning it to punishment by removing its protections and the benefit of rain so that it would be destroyed (verses 5, 6). Only at this point does the Lord identify the offending vineyard:

For the vineyard of the LORD of hosts
    is the house of Israel,
and the men of Judah
    are his pleasant planting (verse 7).

Isaiah 5 goes on to identify the "wild grapes" (verse 4) produced by God's people as a result of their rejection of Him and His law. The fruit of rejection included greed, social injustice, drunkenness, and revelry without regard for God's actions, treating evil as good and good as evil, and conceit (verses 7, 8, 11, 12, 18–24; see also the sins and divine judgment described earlier in Isaiah 2:6–4:1). Therefore, there is no reason for the "vineyard" to continue. God's faithless people would be humbled, invaded, exiled, and destroyed (Isaiah 5:9, 10, 13–17, 25–30).

How much should God do for people before He lets them go? He answers with a rhetorical question, "What more was there to do for my vineyard, that I have not done in it?" (verse 4). The answer is that God continues to work for people and do everything He can for them until there is nothing more that He can do. He does not want anyone to perish (see 2 Peter 3:9). But when He runs out of options for saving them, He abandons them to their fate.

In the near future, the Lord will reach this point with the entire "vineyard" of this world, when its inhabitants will have made and settled into their choices for Him by accepting His "seal" (Revelation 7:2, 3) or against Him by accepting the "mark" of His enemy (Revelation 13:16, 17, NET). At that time, the words will be pronounced: "Let the evildoer still do evil, and the filthy still be filthy, and the righteous still do right, and the holy still be holy" (Revelation 22:11).

God gives free choice, allowing everyone to be the kind of people that they want to be. He does not force us, trick us, or leave us in ignorance but lovingly reveals the full consequences of our options in advance, as He did in Isaiah's day.

There is no good reason why anyone should be lost because "God so loved the world, that he gave his only Son, that whoever believes in him should not perish but have eternal life" (John 3:16). Jesus gave up His exalted identity, humbling himself to become a human being, and suffered the worst death (Philippians 2:5–8) to set us free from the deadly results of our own failures (Galatians 3:10–13). This grand freedom gives us a new identity as the sons and daughters of God (2 Corinthians 6:18). What more could He do?

So who do *you* want to be?

---

1. Jennifer Bellemare, "4 Scary (and Real) Identity Theft Stories," IdentityForce, October 18, 2016, https://www.identityforce.com/blog/4-scary-real-identity-theft-stories.

2. Ana Bera, "50 Shocking Identity Theft Statistics—2020 Update," Safe at Last, February 5, 2019, https://safeatlast.co/blog/identity-theft-statistics/.

3. This occurred after the reign of Uzziah (792–740 BC), whether resulting from the war with Syria and northern Israel during the reign of Ahaz about 735 BC (2 Kings 16; 2 Chronicles 28; Isaiah 7) or the invasion by Sennacherib of Assyria during Hezekiah's reign in 701 BC (Isaiah 36, 37; 2 Kings 18, 19; 2 Chronicles 32). Thus, Isaiah 1 could have been written later than chapters 2–5, which appear to reflect the prosperity that prevailed during the time of Uzziah.

4. For the perspectives of the Hebrew prophets regarding sacrifices and other worship activities, see Roy E. Gane, "Sacrifice and Atonement," in *Dictionary of the Old Testament: Prophets*, ed. Mark J. Boda and J. Gordon McConville (Downers Grove, IL: IVP Academic, 2012), 685–692, especially 688.

5. Wikipedia, s.v. "Michael Cicconetti," last modified February 10, 2020, https://en.wikipedia.org/wiki/Michael_Cicconetti; "Woman Ordered to Spend Night in Woods for Abandoning Kittens," ABC News, November 23, 2005, https://abcnews.go.com/GMA/LegalCenter/story?id=1322751.

6. See Ludwig Koehler, Walter Baumgartner, and Johann J. Stamm, *The Hebrew and Aramaic Lexicon of the Old Testament*, trans. and ed. Mervyn E. J. Richardson, vol. 2 (Leiden: Brill, 1995), 410.

7. Max Lucado, *When God Whispers Your Name* (Dallas: Word, 1994), 52.

8. Ellen G. White, *Thoughts From the Mount of Blessing* (Mountain View, CA: Pacific Press®, 1999), 114.

Two

Who Will Go for God?

Isaiah 6

"O king, live forever!" The expression of this wish was a proper way to address a monarch in ancient times (Daniel 2:4; 3:9). Unlike most presidents today, kings faced no elections and had no term limits. So "live forever" meant "reign forever."

But of course, all kings die. Uzziah, whom the Bible also calls Azariah, was no exception. After a long, stable, and prosperous reign of fifty-two years, he finally passed away in approximately 740 BC (2 Chronicles 26). Isaiah was a young man whose ministry began near the end of Uzziah's reign (Isaiah 1:1), so he had never known anyone but Uzziah as his king. What was going to happen now? There was no parliament or congress, so the fate of Judah depended on the character, capability, and courage of Uzziah's son and successor, Jotham.

Incomparable encounter

But did Judah's fate depend on Jotham? In the same year that Uzziah died, Isaiah saw the real Controller of destinies: "I saw the Lord sitting upon a throne, high and lifted up; and the train of his robe filled the temple" (Isaiah 6:1). Human kings came and went, but here was the only immortal Sovereign,[1] who was all powerful, all seeing, sinless, and pure. This Divine King had His rightful earthly residence in the temple, which was His palace.

By contrast, Uzziah was not even permitted to perform a single priestly act to serve the Lord in the temple. When Uzziah had entered the temple to burn incense on the altar of incense, as if he were an authorized priest, God struck him with the impure disease of leprosy, from which he died (2 Chronicles 26:16–21). Unlike the Divine King, Uzziah was sinful, impure, and mortal.

Human monarchs surround themselves with an aura of glory conveyed through magnificent apparel, glittering objects, monumental structures, many attendants, and pompous ceremonies. Assyrian kings even boasted that their "awesome splendor" overwhelmed their enemies.[2] But their glory was like a children's Christmas pageant compared to that of the Divine King of Israel. No doubt, Isaiah had seen the human king of Judah,[3] but he was not prepared for what he witnessed in his temple vision.

Isaiah could come to the temple courtyard, but he was not permitted to enter the sacred building because he was not a priest. Nevertheless, he saw the Lord in the temple, which implies that this was an interactive visionary experience in which he was inside the temple. In this vision, God was so high and huge that just the lower parts of His robe filled the temple (Isaiah 6:1). As Solomon had said in his prayer when the temple was first dedicated, "But will God indeed dwell on the earth? Behold, heaven and the highest heaven cannot contain you; how much less this house that I have built!" (1 Kings 8:27).

As Isaiah gazed in wonder, he saw the attendants of God: superhuman six-winged seraphim, "fiery ones" (Isaiah 6:2, author's translation), apparently referring to their appearance as glowing like fire.

And one called to another and said:

> "Holy, holy, holy is the LORD of hosts;
> the whole earth is full of his glory!"

And the foundations of the thresholds shook at the voice of him who called, and the house was filled with smoke (verses 3, 4).

The seraphim demonstrated the paramount importance of fully recognizing the incomparable holiness of the Lord, who is the majestic object of worship. He alone is intrinsically holy. Any other holiness of persons, places, or things is secondary, derived from a connection with Him. His holiness encompasses all of His attributes, including but not limited to His uniquely inherent immortality (1 Timothy 6:15, 16), His power to create out of nothing (Genesis 1), His ability to perceive everything (Psalm 139), and His character of unselfish love (1 John 4:8, 16). Because He is the God of love, all "unlove" is His enemy. Unlove is selfishness and selfishness is sin. As the Creator, He is the Source of life, so death that results from sin is alien to Him (Romans 6:23).

If the pure, sinless seraphim of unearthly splendor, who possess such power that their voices of praise shake stone foundations, cover their faces when they are in the presence of the holy Lord of hosts, what reverence should we express when we approach Him, whether in private devotions or in a house of worship? Isaiah reacted by exclaiming, "Woe is me! For I am lost; for I am a man of unclean lips, and I dwell in the midst of a people of unclean lips; for my eyes have seen the King, the LORD of hosts!" (Isaiah 6:5). If the great prophet Isaiah was awestruck and smitten by such a deep sense of unworthiness, how can we respond, except to cry out with him? If he identified as being a sinner among his sinful people (compare Isaiah 1–5;

see also Daniel 9:5–20), can we remain aloof from our sins and shift the blame to others?

Purification by fire

Thankfully for Isaiah and us, God's holy character of love includes mercy for faulty people whose lips are not worthy to praise Him, speak to Him, or tell others about Him. Isaiah states, "Then one of the seraphim flew to me, having in his hand a burning coal that he had taken with tongs from the altar. And he touched my mouth and said: 'Behold, this has touched your lips; your guilt is taken away, and your sin atoned for' " (Isaiah 6:6, 7). This treatment of fire by a fiery seraph was like a baptism with fire (compare Matthew 3:11; Luke 3:16) to purge the mind and conscience of the prophet so that his lips could communicate thoughts in harmony with those of God (compare Jeremiah 1:9).

The fire that purified Isaiah was in the form of a coal from the altar of burnt offering. At the earlier wilderness sanctuary, the Lord Himself had lit the fire on the altar (Leviticus 9:24), which was to be kept continually burning and never go out (Leviticus 6:12, 13 [Hebrew verses 5, 6]). This divine fire consumed the sacrifices offered by the Israelites, through which they received His grace. Even well-being offerings (or "peace offerings") of praise, such as thanksgiving, vow, or freewill offerings (Leviticus 7:12–16) when no atonement for particular sins was needed (compare Leviticus 3 on well-being offerings), required the slaughter of animal victims. These sacrifices pointed forward to the once-for-all, truly effective sacrifice of Christ (John 1:29; Hebrews 9:26; 10:12) on the altar of the cross (Hebrews 13:10–13). Without Christ's sacrifice and priestly intercession, even our praises to God would not be acceptable to Him.[4] No wonder the altar at the Israelite sanctuary and later at the temple was at the center of worship by God's people!

It makes perfect sense that Isaiah would be cleansed by a coal from the altar that prefigured the place of Christ's sacrifice (verses 10–13); His sacrifice is the only means by which human consciences can be purified "from dead works to serve the living God" (Hebrews 9:14; compare Hebrews 10:1–22). It also makes sense that Christ's altar-of-the-cross event is the only valid center of Christian worship (compare 1 Corinthians 2:2). The one who comes to His altar humbly confessing faultiness and calling on God to "be merciful to me, a sinner" (Luke 18:13) can expect to be forgiven and transformed as Isaiah was (1 John 1:9; Titus 3:4–7).

The prayers before sermons in Christian churches quite often petition God to touch the lips of the speaker with a coal from the altar, referring to Isaiah 6. This is an appropriate prayer, but the significance of Isaiah's experience is far wider and deeper. Isaiah was a special speaker for God, and in that sense, he is a model for Christian preachers. But he is also a model for other Christians—all of whom are ministers of the gospel as "a chosen race, a royal priesthood, a holy nation, a people for his own possession, that you may proclaim the excellencies of him who called you out of darkness into his marvelous light" (1 Peter 2:9). Speaking behind a pulpit or in front of a PowerPoint presentation is only one way to speak for God. Talking one-on-one with a neighbor, coworker, or one's child is another way, which may be much more effective for that person. Every Christian needs purified lips, and such lips only come from a purified heart, for "what comes out of the mouth proceeds from the heart" (Matthew 15:18).

Commission from the King

Just after Isaiah received moral cleansing as a divine gift, he heard the Lord's call: "Whom shall I send, and who will go for us?" (Isaiah 6:8). God purifies minds and lips for a purpose, and there is no time to lose when precious people are perishing. Isaiah did not hesitate but immediately replied, "Here I am! Send me" (verse 8). He did not stop to consider the obstacles he might encounter or the hardships he might endure in fulfilling God's commission. He owed everything to his Divine King, whom he implicitly trusted, and it was a privilege and honor to serve Him. The overpowering vision of "the Holy One of Israel" was indelibly etched in his memory[5] and would serve as his guiding light, eclipsing all difficulties.

It appears that Isaiah's prophetic ministry began before his temple vision, described in Isaiah 6, because chapters 2–5 of his book reflect conditions of prosperity that prevailed during the reign of Uzziah (compare 2 Chronicles 26:5–15). If so, his vision confirmed his call and gave his morale and sense of mission a massive and much-needed boost after he had engaged with the spiritual and social rottenness of Judah, especially Jerusalem. Just as Moses requested of the Lord, "Show me your glory" (Exodus 33:18), after the devastating and disheartening golden-calf apostasy (Exodus 32), what Isaiah needed above all was a close encounter with the Divine Presence.

While we have not had Isaiah's visionary experience, God gave it to him for all of us. The Lord is Sovereign—our Source of stability and security when everything in our lives seems uncertain. He is holy, just, and merciful when all around us is defiled, unjust, and cruel. By faith, we can behold Him high and lifted up, "keeping watch above His own."[6]

Isaiah 2:2–4 envisions all nations coming to the Lord's temple to receive His guidance, but in Isaiah 6, the Lord sends Isaiah out of the temple to minister to His people. These are the two basic ways in which God continues to draw the inhabitants of our world to Himself: sending out messengers and pulling people inward to join His attractive community of faith. Thus, Jesus gave us His great commission: "Go therefore and make disciples of all nations" (Matthew 28:19). He also prayed to His Father for unity among His followers: "So that the world may believe that you have sent me" (John 17:21). This unity would draw others in by testifying of a kind of love that only the Lord can give.

Both approaches to mission should work together. God's people must go out in order to reach those who otherwise would never learn of His love and salvation through Christ. But unless Christians are unified and strive to reflect God's character in their lives and social interactions, going out to bring others in will be futile because people will be repelled by a fractured church with unloving members whose lives are hypocritical and discordant with their message. This is why the apostle ("sent one") Paul not only went out on missionary journeys (Acts 13–21) but also labored to heal divisions and dissensions (for example, 1 Corinthians 1–4) and guide church communities in holy living that would properly represent God and bring people in to Him (for example, 1 Corinthians 5–8).

Reality check

After Isaiah's awesome experience with God and direct commission from Him, one could expect his ministry to become one of the most successful in history, converting many thousands to the true worship of God. One could also expect the Lord to provide encouragement to His newly anointed messenger. Shockingly, however, His charge was nothing but depressing:

And he said, "Go, and say to this people:

" 'Keep on hearing, but do not understand;
keep on seeing, but do not perceive.'
Make the heart of this people dull,
and their ears heavy,
and blind their eyes;
lest they see with their eyes,
and hear with their ears,
and understand with their hearts,
and turn and be healed" (Isaiah 6:9, 10).

What a waste of effort! Why bother, especially when your efforts will only make things worse? Maybe Isaiah should have considered another kind of career.

God's words, when taken out of context, raise a question of theodicy—that is, a justification of His character: Why would He send an unprofitable prophet to keep people from understanding in order to prevent them from being saved? How could He claim to be a God of love (1 John 4:8)?

Jesus cited these verses of Isaiah when He explained to His disciples why He taught in parables:

> "This is why I speak to them in parables, because seeing they do not see, and hearing they do not hear, nor do they understand. Indeed, in their case the prophecy of Isaiah is fulfilled that says:
>
> > " ' "You will indeed hear but never understand" ' " (Matthew 13:13, 14).

The meaning of these words becomes clear in John 12, which refers to Isaiah 53:1 and then to Isaiah 6:9, 10:

> Though he [Jesus] had done so many signs before them, they still did not believe in him, so that the word spoken by the prophet Isaiah might be fulfilled:
>
> > "Lord, who has believed what he heard from us,
> > and to whom has the arm of the Lord been revealed?"
>
> Therefore they could not believe. For again, Isaiah said,
>
> > "He has blinded their eyes
> > and hardened their heart,
> > lest they see with their eyes,

and understand with their heart, and turn,
and I would heal them" (John 12:37–40).

Jesus did all He could to help people believe, including the performance of amazing miracles. But they chose not to believe. When they rejected the clear evidence that He offered, the additional evidence that He mercifully provided only resulted in further disbelief, so their lack of faith became more confirmed and hardened. His goal was to save them, but they abused His best efforts so that their spiritual state was worse than if He had not come to them at all.

Jesus' explanation to His disciples followed His parable of the sower, in which the sower scattered his seed in the same way on various kinds of earth (Matthew 13:3–8). The widely divergent results were due only to differences in the nature of the surfaces on which his seed fell; they represent the various kinds of people who hear the "word of the kingdom" (verses 18–23). It was their responses that determined the outcomes. Similarly, God is fair and loving in making "his sun rise on the evil and on the good" (Matthew 5:45). But the sun can cause opposing effects, depending on what its rays reach. For example, the same sun melts ice but hardens concrete; likewise, the preaching by Isaiah and Jesus had a hardening effect on people's hearts, similar to the effect that the ten plagues had on the pharaoh of Egypt (on the pharaoh, see Exodus 7:13, 14, 22, etc.). Everyone has free choice, and in the end, nobody in the universe will be able to accuse God of not doing everything He could to save lost souls (Isaiah 5:4).

The Lord was merciful in revealing to Isaiah at the outset that his success would not be in human responses of mortal kings like Uzziah, Jotham, and Ahaz, but in faithfulness to his divine mission. Similarly, Christ has commissioned His followers to proclaim "this gospel of the kingdom . . . throughout the whole world as a testimony to all nations, and then the end will come" (Matthew 24:14). His desire and ours is for everyone to receive His salvation, but the work will be successful and completed when the message has effectively gone "as a testimony," whether people accept it or not (see Ezekiel 2:5, 7; 3:11).

Naturally, Isaiah wondered how long the Judahites' unresponsiveness would continue. The Lord answered that it would go on until the cities and land would be devastated and the people exiled (Isaiah 6:11–13). In other words, most of the Judahites would not repent, so the nation would feel the full force of the covenant curses presented in Leviticus 26 and Deuteronomy 28, which climax with national destruction and exile. The only hope would be a remnant "stump" that would be a "holy seed" with potential for new growth (Isaiah 6:13; compare Daniel 4:15, 26). The theme of this prophecy—destruction and exile but the restoration of a remnant—is developed throughout the book of Isaiah; it also was encapsulated in the name of one of Isaiah's sons: *Shear-jashub*, which means "a remnant will return" (Isaiah 7:3).

Who will go for God? Isaiah went anyway. Will you?

---

1. The word translated "the Lord" here in Isa. 6:1 and also in verses 8, 11 is the title *'adonay*, not His proper name *YHWH*, which modern scholars often read as *Yahweh* (*Jehovah* in some English versions, especially older ones). Most current English versions translate *YHWH* as if it were a title: "the Lord" (as in verses 3, 5, 12).

2. See, for example, Mordechai Cogan, trans., "Sennacherib's Siege of Jerusalem," in *The Context of Scripture*, ed. William W. Hallo, vol. 2 (Leiden: Brill, 1997), 2.119B:302, 303.

3. Jewish tradition even maintains that Isaiah's father Amoz (Isaiah 1:1; 2:1; 13:1; etc.) was the brother of King Amaziah, who was the father of King Uzziah (Babylonian Talmud, Megilla 10b; Sotah 10b).

4. Compare Ellen G. White, *Selected Messages*, bk. 1 (Washington, DC: Review and Herald®, 1958), 344.

5. See this expression throughout the book of Isaiah—for example, in Isaiah 10:20; 12:6; 17:7; 29:19; 30:11, 12, 15.

6. James Russell Lowell, "Once to Every Man and Nation," in *The Seventh-day Adventist Hymnal* (Hagerstown, MD: Review and Herald®, 2006), hymn no. 606.

Three

Whom Do You Trust?
Isaiah 7

King Ahaz was a member of the dynasty established by David. He was the son of Jotham, who was the son of Uzziah. Shortly before Uzziah died (about 740 BC), Tiglath-pileser III began to reign over Assyria in 745 BC. This king sought to expand his domain greatly by conquering other nations. Faced with the imminent prospect of annihilation by the Assyrian superpower, the kingdoms of Syria and northern Israel made an alliance to fight Assyria. These neighboring kingdoms had fought against each other many times (for example, 1 Kings 20; 2 Kings 6; 13), but now a greater danger united them.

Syria and Israel needed support from Judah to the south, but Judah was far from Assyria and did not want to get involved. Syria and Israel were desperate, so they were unwilling to take no for an answer. They decided to take Judah by force, depose its king—namely, Ahaz—and set up a puppet ruler who would cooperate with them (Isaiah 7:1, 5, 6). So they marched their armies to Jerusalem, the capital of Judah, and besieged it (2 Kings 16:5). Never before had a coalition of Israel and Syria threatened the very existence of the Davidic dynasty in Judah.

Declaration of dependence

Ahaz was young and inexperienced. He had come to the throne quite recently at the age of twenty (verse 2), and this was a terrifying crisis because deposed kings had short life expectancies. Isaiah graphically describes the reaction of the Judahite royal court: "The heart of Ahaz and the heart of his people shook as the trees of the forest shake before the wind" (Isaiah 7:2).

The Syrian-Israelite siege of Jerusalem was not succeeding in conquering the city (2 Kings 16:5; Isaiah 7:1), but Ahaz did not want to take any chances. So he sent a rich bribe to Tiglath-pileser III, the king of Assyria, along with a message saying, "I am your servant and your son. Come up and rescue me from the hand of the king of Syria and from the hand of the king of Israel, who are attacking me" (2 Kings 16:7). The Assyrian king happily complied. In 734 BC, he marched his army to Damascus, the capital of Syria, besieged and took it, carried its inhabitants away captive, and killed the Syrian king (verse 9). So ended the kingdom of Syria and the Syrian-Israelite threat to Judah.

Hooray for Ahaz! What a brilliant move! But a price came with the bribe. Both Tiglath-pileser and Ahaz knew what Ahaz meant when he introduced his appeal with the words "I am your servant and your son." This was a declaration of dependence. Ahaz was placing himself under the protection of the Assyrian king as his subordinate. He was giving up Judah's independence to the domination and influence of the ruthlessly cruel Assyrian pagan power, from which there could be no easy escape. As 2 Chronicles 28 describes the situation, bribing the Assyrian king "did not help him" (verse 21) because "Tiglath-pileser king of Assyria came against him and afflicted him instead of strengthening him" (verse 20).

The rest of the story

Now for the rest of the story. Events did not need to turn out like that! It was not necessary for Judah to lose its independence, subject itself to Assyria's support and manipulation, pay tribute to it, and be under its dangerous, corrupting influence. God knew better, and He would have protected Ahaz and Judah if only Ahaz would have trusted Him and exercised the courage that comes from faith.

Before Ahaz appealed to Tiglath-pileser, the Lord sent His prophet Isaiah to Ahaz to dissuade him from making this bad mistake, instead assuring him that the threat from Syria and northern Israel would soon melt anyway, without the need to involve Assyria. Tiglath-pileser did not need a bribe to attack Syria and Israel any more than Hitler needed a bribe to attack Poland in 1939; his path of conquest was already heading in that direction.

"And the LORD said to Isaiah, 'Go out to meet Ahaz, you and Shear-jashub your son, at the end of the conduit of the upper pool on the highway to the Washer's Field' " (Isaiah 7:3). The location "at the end of the conduit of the upper pool" suggests that Ahaz would be inspecting Jerusalem's water supply, which would be crucial during a siege.

When Isaiah would introduce his son to Ahaz, Shear-jashub's name would give Ahaz chills. The name *Shear-jashub* means "a remnant will return." It could mean that a remnant of the people would return to the Lord—that is, they would repent and be converted (compare Isaiah 1:27; 10:21; Jeremiah 3:12). Alternatively, it could mean that a remnant would return from battle or from exile (compare Nehemiah 8:17; Jeremiah 30:10) or survive destruction (Isaiah 10:22). This name could be a conditional prophetic warning that only some would return if God's people did not repent; simultaneously, it could be a harbinger of hope that there would be subsequent restoration for the few. Isaiah's young son was a living, breathing, and walking conditional message and appeal. He was a promise that God controlled the fate of Judah.

By taking Shear-jashub to meet the king, according to the Lord's command, Isaiah honored his son. This action may have sent Ahaz an implicit rebuke by presenting a radical contrast to the way he treated his own son: "He made his son pass through the fire, according to the abominations of the nations whom the LORD had cast out from before the children of Israel" (2 Kings 16:3, NKJV; prohibited in Deuteronomy 18:10; Leviticus 18:21; 20:1–5).

But Isaiah's message to Ahaz from the Lord was clear: do not be afraid because the plot to overthrow Judah will not succeed (Isaiah 7:4–9a). Judah's Syrian and northern Israelite enemies were on the way out, like mere smoldering stumps of firebrands. Then came God's appeal to Ahaz and the members of his court, including his family: "If you [plural] are not firm in faith, you [plural] will not be firm at all" (verse 9b). If you will not trust Me, you will not endure.

Everything depended on trust in God. Such trust is built by experience with Him. One who has believed in Him and has followed His word and found it to be reliable can trust Him when a crisis comes and there is nothing to depend on but His word (compare Genesis 22; see also Hebrews 11:17–19).

Tragically, Ahaz was not such a person. He was further away from God and rebelled against Him more than any king of Judah up to that point (2 Kings 16:2–4; 2 Chronicles 28:1–4). Ahaz was an idolatrous polytheist, not a true worshiper of the one Lord, whom he did not trust or obey.

Ahaz was responsible for bringing upon his nation and himself the crisis of the Syrian-Israelite coalition. Because of his sins, God allowed the Syrians and northern Israelites to defeat the armies of Judah in battle, killing numerous Judahites and taking many captive (2 Chronicles 28:5–15; see also verses 17–19).

We can see two reasons why God did this. First, He could not continue to pour His covenant blessings on people who were unfaithful to Him, or He would send the wrong message to the world—namely, that loyalty to Him as the covenant Lord did not matter. Second, God's discipline was an attempt to awaken Ahaz and the Judahites to the reality that their well-being and existence depended on Him. If they did not cooperate with Him, they were on their own in a cruel and dangerous world.

God's people were object lessons to teach the world the results of loyalty or disloyalty to Him. His ways did not change. He wanted to bestow lavish blessings on His faithful people in order to attract the attention of others and draw them to Himself. But He could not do this if they ignored His instructions.

An offer too good to refuse

Ahaz deserved nothing but death for idolatry, the murder of his own children, and high treason against the Divine King, which had resulted in the deaths of thousands of his soldiers in battle (see 2 Chronicles 28:6). But after God reduced Ahaz's options through defeat and brought him to a critical crisis point, in which he stared death in the face, the Lord gave this miserable, faithless wretch an astounding offer to help him believe that what Isaiah told him about the end of the Syrian-Israelite threat would surely come to pass: "Ask a sign of the LORD your God; let it be deep as Sheol [the underworld; place of the dead] or high as heaven" (Isaiah 7:11). Anything that Ahaz asked, God would do just to prove that He could, including save the king from his enemies. This was a no-risk blank check for Ahaz to fill in any amount that he wished. How many of us would love to have such an opportunity!

Shockingly, Ahaz turned down God's offer (verse 12)! He was not even willing to give the Lord a chance to persuade him by providing a way of escape (compare 1 Corinthians 10:13) because he was entrenched in unbelief and the kind of life that went with it and thus did not want to change. Faith in God would bring an acknowledgment of His lordship and Ahaz's accountability to Him, which he did not want. He wanted to be in charge, no matter what. God had already shown him the futility of that course by reducing his kingdom—what he was in charge of.

Isaiah's next words to Ahaz, and now also to the royal household, were ominous: "Hear then, O house of David! Is it too little for you to weary men, that you weary my God also?" (verse 13). In verse 11, the Lord, through Isaiah, addressed Ahaz: "Ask a sign of the Lord *your* God" (emphasis added). Now Isaiah said that "you weary *my* God" (emphasis added). By rejecting this opportunity for faith, Ahaz had rejected the Lord as his God. The Lord was the God of Isaiah but not of Ahaz and his household.

To weary God is dangerous. When He is (metaphorically) weary from giving appeals that are only rejected, He is approaching the point where there is nothing more that He can do to help (compare Isaiah 5:4).

Isaiah could be reasonably expected to issue Ahaz a divine verdict of inescapable, impending disaster, which he did, but mixed with it was a message of hope for God's people. Ahaz had refused a sign, but the Lord would give him a sign anyway:

"Look, this young woman is about to conceive and will give birth to a son. You, young woman, will name him Immanuel. He will eat sour milk and honey, which will help him know how to reject evil and choose what is right. Here is why this will be so: Before the child knows how to reject evil and choose what is right, the land whose two kings you fear will be desolate. The Lord will bring on you, your people, and your father's family a time unlike any since Ephraim departed from Judah—the king of Assyria!" (Isaiah 7:14–17, NET).

The good news was that the land of Syria and northern Israel ("the land whose two kings you dread" [verse 16]) would be deserted, so these nations would cease to threaten Judah. This would happen in a short amount of time, even before a baby boy who was to be born soon would be old enough to choose what food he liked and what he did not want to eat. The bad news was that the king of Assyria was coming. He—the very one to whom Ahaz was about to appeal for help—was the real threat.

The sign of Immanuel made two points. First, his name, *Immanuel*, means "God is with us" (a verbless sentence in Hebrew, for which the word *is* should be supplied). Whether Ahaz liked it or not, the Lord was still with His people and directed their destiny. For a believer in God, this sign of His continuing presence would provide comfort and hope. Second, the boy's development provided a time frame within which key events would occur. It appears that the boy would eat sour milk, or curds, and honey because crops of grains, fruits, and vegetables would be lacking due to the devastation of the land.

The Bible does not identify this Immanuel or his mother, who is described in Isaiah 7:14 simply as an *'almah*—"a young woman or girl of marriageable age."[1] Elsewhere in the Bible, the Hebrew word can refer to unmarried virgins (sexually uninitiated) in contexts where this level of detail can be determined (Genesis 24:43; Exodus 2:8), but in other cases, the young women may not be virgins in this sense (Song of Solomon 1:3; 6:8; Proverbs 30:19, which could refer to sexual experience). So perhaps this girl was about to get married and then become pregnant when Isaiah spoke to Ahaz. Alternatively, it is possible that the term *'almah* could include a recently married young woman. If so, Immanuel's mother may have already been pregnant (compare NJPS: "Look, the young woman is with child"; Isaiah 7:14). In any case, like Isaiah's son Shear-jashub, the boy Immanuel was a prophetic sign for Ahaz.

Yet Immanuel's significance went much further because he

served as a type—a historical prefiguration to which a later and much greater salvific reality would correspond.[2] Centuries later, a young woman would miraculously conceive by the Holy Spirit while she was still an unmarried virgin. An angel informed her fiancé Joseph:

> "She will bear a son, and you shall call his name Jesus, for he will save his people from their sins." All this took place to fulfill what the Lord had spoken by the prophet:
>
> > "Behold, the virgin shall conceive and bear a son,
> >   and they shall call his name Immanuel"
>
> (which means, God with us) (Matthew 1:21–23).

Here the Greek text of Matthew quotes from the Septuagint translation of Isaiah 7:14, which translates the Hebrew *'almah* as the Greek *parthenos*, denoting a virgin in the technical sense of "one who has never engaged in sexual intercourse."[3]

The name *Jesus* is a shortened form of *Joshua*, which means "YHWH [the personal name of Israel's God] is salvation." As mentioned above, *Immanuel* means "God is with us" (the verb *is* was implied in the Hebrew but was left out in the literal Greek translation in Matthew 1:23). The names *Jesus* and *Immanuel* are powerful promises that are related to each other. Jesus, the Son of God, can save us from our sins and their fatal results because He has come in human flesh, "born of woman" (Galatians 4:4), to bring God's presence to us not only for a few years but for all time.

The Lord offered Ahaz a sign; it could be as "deep as Sheol or high as heaven" (Isaiah 7:11). In Jesus, God has given us a sign that is "high as heaven" to rescue us from subjection to the cruel "ruler of this world" (John 12:31), whose evil is as "deep as Sheol." Jesus said, "If you abide in my word, you are truly my disciples, and you will know the truth, and the truth will set you free" (John 8:31, 32).

Ahaz refused to abide in God's word or know the truth; instead, he trusted himself and lost his freedom by choosing a cruel master.

Whom do you trust?

---

1. See Ludwig Koehler and Walter Baumgartner, *The Hebrew and Aramaic Lexicon of the Old Testament*, vol. 2, trans. and ed. M. E. J. Richardson (Leiden: Brill, 2000), 835, 836.

2. For a definition of biblical typology and controls for identifying types in the Old Testament, see Richard M. Davidson, "The Eschatological Hermeneutic of Biblical Typology," *TheoRhēma* 6, no. 2 (2011): 5–48.

3. Frederick W. Danker, Walter Bauer, William F. Arndt, and F. Wilbur Gingrich, *A Greek-English Lexicon of the New Testament and Other Early Christian Literature*, 3rd. ed. (Chicago: University of Chicago Press, 2000), 777.

Four

Whom Do You Fear?
Isaiah 8

Isaiah and his wife did not need to find a name for their new baby. Even before their son was conceived, God told them what to name him: Maher-shalal-hash-baz (Isaiah 8:1). This long name means "the spoil speeds, the prey hastens."[1] The boy's childhood development was prophetic: "For before the boy knows how to cry 'My father' or 'My mother,' the wealth of Damascus and the spoil of Samaria will be carried away before the king of Assyria" (verse 4).

The prophecy of Maher-shalal-hash-baz reinforced Isaiah's prediction regarding the demise of the northern Israelite–Syrian alliance, as signified by the birth and development of the boy Immanuel: "He shall eat curds and honey when he knows how to refuse the evil and choose the good. For before the boy knows how to refuse the evil and choose the good, the land whose two kings you dread will be deserted" (Isaiah 7:15, 16).

That was good news, but Ahaz's lack of faith would bring a much greater danger for Judah: the Assyrian superpower (Isaiah 8:5–8; compare Isaiah 7:17–20). Nevertheless, the military might and plotting of the enemies of Immanuel and his people, implicitly including the Assyrians, would not last (Isaiah 8:9,

10; compare Isaiah 7:7), "for God is with us" (Isaiah 8:10). So the Judahites should learn from their bitter experience and trust in God to deliver them.

Isaiah gives his personal testimony: "I will wait for the LORD, who is hiding his face from the house of Jacob, and I will hope in him" (verse 17). Centuries earlier, God had commanded His priests to pronounce a blessing on the Israelites, which included the following words: "The LORD make his face to shine upon you and be gracious to you; the LORD lift up his countenance upon you and give you peace" (Numbers 6:25, 26). But now He was hiding His face—a sign of disfavor and that He was withholding blessing (see Isaiah 54:8; 57:17; 59:2; 64:7 [Hebrew verse 6]). Nevertheless, Isaiah cherished the hope that this was temporary because he knew that God's love is "everlasting" (Isaiah 54:8).

If the people of Judah doubted God at this point, they would later learn from Isaiah's written prophecies that the Lord had history and providence firmly in His big hands all along. Therefore, Isaiah certified and safeguarded an official record of his prophetic teaching among his disciples (Isaiah 8:16) so that it could serve as a credible witness to judgment and hope in the future.

The balance between judgment and hope permeated the messages of the Hebrew prophets, and it enabled a remnant of God's people to survive. Such balance is needed today more than ever. On the one hand, we see an epidemic of despair, with suicide rates soaring. People desperately need hope—hope that will save their lives. On the other hand, many feel no accountability to anyone or anything but themselves. Such persons need a sense of judgment, which is part of God's gospel (good news) because it calls them to submit to Him, the Creator, who is the only Source of life (Revelation 14:6, 7).

Both hope and judgment are needed in people's lives. Hope keeps us going, and judgment keeps us from going off track. Without hope, we give up on the possibility of progress; without judgment, we end up in a "train wreck." One major sickness of our age is that many people refuse corrections that would help them; instead, they claim to be too sensitive (about themselves, although not necessarily others) and are easily discouraged.

Fearing the right thing

Fear is a powerful motivator that we need to keep us alive. For example, if you accidentally drop your mobile phone onto the track of a subway train, what keeps you from jumping down on the track to retrieve it? Fear. Subway trains are good, but we know what they can do to us if we fail to respect their boundaries. Fear of the right thing is good.

Misplaced fear can be problematic, especially if it causes you to overlook or underestimate a greater danger. For example, fear of a stinging insect in your car while you are driving could distract you so that while you are attempting to swat the insect, you lose control of the vehicle and have an accident. Some fear is simply false. Scammers use lies to prey on people by threatening dire consequences if they do not reveal personal information or pay money. Fabricated conspiracy theories generate wrong attitudes and harmful decisions. Fear of the wrong thing is bad. So we should evaluate decisions and their potential dangers, making conscious choices, rather than impulsive responses.

Isaiah was faced with various dangers, so the Lord warned him to fear the right thing: "For the LORD spoke thus to me with his strong hand upon me, and warned me not to walk in the way of this people, saying: 'Do not call conspiracy all that this people calls conspiracy, and do not fear what they fear, nor be in dread. But the LORD of hosts, him you shall honor as holy. Let him be your fear, and let him be your dread' " (Isaiah 8:11–13).

God commanded Isaiah to fear Him rather than human threats, indicating that fear is not only an emotion but also a choice. The Judahites feared the wrong things, including such conspiracies as the plots against them by the leaders of Syria and northern Israel (Isaiah 7:5, 6). Even if conspiracies are real, they can distract people from more significant dangers, such as Assyria, in the case of Judah. Human conspiracies, whether they concern national or church politics, can absorb modern Christians, making them lose faith in divine power to protect them and ensnaring them in Satan's schemes to separate them from God. It is easy to fear what everyone else fears, but God's true people should look higher—to Him.

For Isaiah, there was no comparison between the earth-shaking power and glory of God (Isaiah 6) and any threatening force that puny human beings could muster. So he had no reason to fear the earthly troubles that his fellow citizens feared.

Alternative "facts"

What do faithless people do when they crave knowledge of future events but dislike the knowledge that God gives? One option is to seek alternative, occult sources of knowledge, as King Saul did (1 Samuel 28).

Even if some information from an occult source turns out to be factual, the source of the information is still dangerous. Trusting anything other than God's Word places one under the deadly influence of satanic power. Therefore, biblical law categorically rules out occult sources of knowledge (Exodus 22:18 [Hebrew verse 17]; Leviticus 19:26, 31; 20:6, 27; Deuteronomy 18:9–14).

King Ahaz was a practicing pagan (2 Kings 16:3, 4). Although the Bible does not explicitly state that he resorted to occult knowledge (as it says of King Manasseh in 2 Chronicles 33:6), it is likely that he and others in Judah were at least tempted to do so. Two factors reinforce this possibility. First, pagan religion is occult in nature. Deuteronomy 32:17 and 1 Corinthians 10:20 characterize pagan sacrifices as sacrifices to demons. So it would be a small step for someone like Ahaz, who offered pagan sacrifices (2 Kings 16:3, 4), to seek occult knowledge. Second, Isaiah makes a point of strongly condemning occult mediums in a way that seems to warn Ahaz: "And when they say to you, 'Inquire of the mediums and the necromancers who chirp and mutter,' should not a people inquire of their God? Should they inquire of the dead on behalf of the living? To the teaching and to the testimony! If they will not speak according to this word, it is because they have no dawn" (Isaiah 8:19, 20).

"This word" is "the teaching" and "the testimony," referring in reverse (chiastic) order to the prophetic "testimony" and "teaching" of Isaiah (verse 16). The people of Judah had the magnificent oracles of the Living God, so there was no good reason for them to go after the chirpings and mutterings of spiritists.

It does not make sense to "inquire of the dead on behalf of the living" (verse 19) because "the dead know nothing" (Ecclesiastes 9:5). Therefore, if you think you can communicate with a dead relative who loved you in order to receive wise counsel and reliable information, you are being fooled and trapped.

Those who fail to speak in harmony with God's Word "have no dawn." In other words, they remain in perpetual darkness (Isaiah 8:22), which can be interpreted as spiritual, mental, and emotional darkness and despair that are accompanied by distress, hunger (or emptiness), rage, and curses against their king and their God or gods (verse 21).

Occult influences are flooding our modern world, and society is becoming increasingly dangerous as a result. Our only safety is in God's teaching and testimony, which give us hope and instruct us where to place our fear.

Whom do you fear?

---

1. David J. A. Clines, ed., *The Dictionary of Classical Hebrew*, vol. 5, *Mem–Nun* (Sheffield, UK: Sheffield Phoenix Press, 2001), 168.

Five

Why Sing for Joy?
Isaiah 9, 11, 12

One of the most exciting and joyful moments of married life is learning that a baby is on the way. All kinds of thoughts trip over each other as they rush together: *When is the baby due? Will it be a boy or a girl? What will we name the baby? How will our lives change? What will this new person become?*

God with us
Imagine the excitement and joy brought by the birth announcement recorded in Isaiah 9:

> For to us a child is born,
>> to us a son is given;
> and the government shall be upon his shoulder,
>> and his name shall be called
> Wonderful Counselor, Mighty God,
>> Everlasting Father, Prince of Peace (verse 6
>> [Hebrew verse 5]).

The boy will have not just one name with special meaning, such as Isaiah's sons Shear-jashub and Maher-shalal-hash-baz

(Isaiah 7:3; 8:1, 3), but several amazing names. He will radically change lives for the better as a mighty leader.

The child in Isaiah 9 will become literally "a wonder of a counselor" (or "a wonder, a counselor"); he will possess supreme wisdom so that he will always know the right thing to do in any situation. In the biblical world, a counselor could be an advisor to a king (2 Samuel 15:12; Isaiah 19:11), but this child will be the king (Isaiah 9:7 [Hebrew verse 6]), having the power to carry out his wise decisions. Elsewhere in the Bible, the Hebrew word for "wonder" often refers to something outside the realm of ordinary possibility, such as a miracle that only God can perform (for example, Exodus 15:11; Psalm 78:12; Isaiah 25:1). Another word from the same Hebrew root appears in Judges 13:18, when the angel (messenger) of the Lord replied to Manoah, the father of Samson, who had asked for the angel's name: "Why do you ask my name, seeing it is wonderful?"

The next two names of the child in Isaiah 9 are stunning: "Mighty God, Everlasting Father" (verse 6 [Hebrew verse 5]). It would be utterly blasphemous for a human being to have these names—unless the child is God incarnate, the Creator, and therefore the ultimate Father of everyone in human form! He will be born as a new human, the Son of God, but His origin "is from of old, from ancient days" (Micah 5:2). He will be the ultimate Immanuel, "God is with us" (Isaiah 7:14).[1]

The Son will be the "Prince of Peace" (Isaiah 9:6). The Hebrew word translated "Peace" involves much more than an absence of conflict; it includes prosperity, well-being, and safety. This Leader will bring well-being, and He will establish and uphold His rule "with justice and with righteousness" forever (verse 7 [Hebrew verse 6]), unlike the selfish, unjust, and corrupt princes in Jerusalem, whom Isaiah had previously described (Isaiah 1:23).

The Divine Son will reign forever as King "on the throne of David," continuing his dynasty. Rather than presiding over a progressively shrinking kingdom, as the royal descendants of David have done, the new Son will have a government that will continually increase (Isaiah 9:7 [Hebrew verse 6]).

Identifying the Wonder Child

For centuries, no leader came close to matching Isaiah's description. Then a descendant of David was born in Bethlehem (Matthew 2:1), David's town of origin (1 Samuel 16), fulfilling the prophecy of Micah (Micah 5:2; Matthew 2:6), who was a contemporary of Isaiah. The Son was "born king of the Jews" (Matthew 2:2). His mother was a virgin, and His biological Father was the Holy Spirit; therefore, He was literally the "Son of God" (Luke 1:35) and "Immanuel"—"God is with us" (Isaiah 7:14; Matthew 1:23). An angel announced His birth as "good news of great joy that will be for all the people" because He is "a Savior, who is Christ the Lord" (Luke 2:10, 11). Then a heavenly multitude praised God: "Glory to God in the highest, and on earth peace, goodwill toward men!" (verse 14, NKJV). This Jesus, who "will save His people from their sins" (Matthew 1:21, NKJV), can be none other than the divine, royal Child of whom Isaiah spoke, who "became flesh and dwelt among us" (John 1:14).

Christ (Greek *Christos*, meaning "Anointed One" or "Messiah," from the Hebrew *mashiakh*) began His ministry in the region of Galilee. According to Matthew 4:14–16, this fulfilled the prophecy recorded in the beginning of Isaiah 9:

> But there will be no gloom for her who was in anguish. In the former time he brought into contempt the land of Zebulun and the land of Naphtali, but in the latter time he has made glorious the way of the sea, the land beyond the Jordan, Galilee of the nations.

> The people who walked in darkness
>> have seen a great light;
> those who dwelt in a land of deep darkness,
>> on them has light shone (Isaiah 9:1, 2 [Hebrew verses 8:23–9:1]).

The words "but there will be no gloom" are in contrast to the description of the hopeless ones who rely on occult sources of knowledge rather than on God's sure word (Isaiah 8:22). Indeed, the failure of the northern kingdom of Israel to listen to the Lord led to its conquest by the Assyrians (2 Kings 17:5–18). The first area of Israel to fall included Galilee, with all the land of the tribe of Naphtali (2 Kings 15:29).

Centuries later, the gloom of Galilee was broken by "a great light" (Isaiah 9:2), the "true light, which gives light to everyone" (John 1:9). Jesus "went throughout all Galilee, teaching in their synagogues and proclaiming the gospel of the kingdom and healing every disease and every affliction among the people" (Matthew 4:23). The first region that had fallen captive was now the first to hear of freedom through Christ, who was establishing His new kingdom of heaven on earth. He offered the peace of personal and social well-being, as shown by His healing ministry and His teaching of divine principles (for example, Matthew 5–7). More than that, this Prince of Peace came to give "peace with God" through the sacrifice of Himself (Romans 4:25–5:1; compare Hebrews 7:27; 9:26). The coming of the Child born to and for us would be the beginning of the end of the forces of darkness.

A new David

The Lord chose David, the youngest son of Jesse, to be anointed as king over Israel (1 Samuel 16). With divine blessing and protection, David overcame great obstacles to defeat the enemies of God's people and build a mighty empire. David made some serious mistakes (especially 2 Samuel 11; 24), but overall, he ruled faithfully and justly according to divine principles (1 Kings 3:6; 9:4).

The Davidic dynasty deteriorated during the following centuries until it could be likened to a mere "stump of Jesse" (Isaiah 11:1), rather than a magnificent fruit-bearing tree (Daniel 4). This situation sounds like the end of the story. But no, even a stump can harbor new life. As the Lord told Isaiah regarding his country, which would be devastated like a tree that is felled, "The holy seed is its stump" (Isaiah 6:13).

Isaiah 11 predicts the rise of someone who would be like David:

> There shall come forth a shoot from the stump of Jesse,
>   and a branch from his roots shall bear fruit.
> And the Spirit of the LORD shall rest upon him,
>   the Spirit of wisdom and understanding,
>   the Spirit of counsel and might,
>   the Spirit of knowledge and the fear of the LORD
>   (verses 1, 2).

He would not be merely another descendant of David but would come "from the stump of Jesse," implying that He is a new David. He would be righteous and faithful to the Lord, following just principles to give judgments for the benefit of poor and vulnerable people. But He would destroy the wicked (verses 3–5). His role as the Judge who destroys the wicked identifies him as a King (compare Psalm 101:5, 8).

David exerted his power through military and political force, but the "shoot from the stump of Jesse" would "strike the earth with the rod of his mouth, and with the breath of his lips he shall kill the wicked" (Isaiah 11:4). Whose words could pack that kind of a punch? This sounds like divine power. Just as startling and confirming of His divine power, the peacefulness of His leadership ultimately would extend even to nature. Predatory animals would cease to eat weaker species; rather, they would harmlessly coexist with them (verses 6–9). If even this can happen, it implies that humans especially will stop preying on one another, and conflict will be no more (compare Isaiah 2:4).

"In that day the root of Jesse, who shall stand as a signal for the peoples—of him shall the nations inquire, and his resting place shall be glorious" (Isaiah 11:10). This verse refers to the same period of time when the "shoot from the stump of Jesse" (verse 1)—that is, a descendant of Jesse—will reign. But here in verse 10, the same Person is paradoxically called "the root of Jesse," which reveals that He is a forefather of Jesse. The fact that nations would be drawn to inquire of Him indicates that He is an internationally recognized source of wise counsel (compare Isaiah 2:2–4).

Let us add up the characteristics of the new David: a King descended from Jesse—and therefore from David—upon whom "the Spirit of counsel" rests (Isaiah 11:2), who possesses divine power, who is also an ancestor of Jesse and David, and who brings peace. These attributes fit the description of the Child announced by Isaiah 9, who would rule forever "on the throne of David" (Isaiah 9:7 [Hebrew verse 6]).

Therefore, the Messianic prophecy in Isaiah 11 must also point to Jesus Christ. This is confirmed by Romans 15:12, where Paul applies Isaiah's prophecy of "the root of Jesse" (Isaiah 11:10) to Christ. In Revelation 19, from the mouth of One called "The Word of God" (verse 13), who is Christ (compare John 1), "comes a sharp sword with which to strike down the nations, and he will rule them with a rod of iron" (Revelation 19:15; compare Isaiah 11:4). In Revelation 22:16, Jesus calls Himself both "the root [ancestor] and the descendant of David."

After the message of hope in Isaiah 11, Isaiah 12 breaks into a song of praise:

"I will give thanks to you, O Lord,
   for though you were angry with me,
your anger turned away,
   that you might comfort me.

"Behold, God is my salvation;
   I will trust, and will not be afraid;
for the Lord God is my strength and my song" (verses 1, 2).

This is our song too. God's justified anger against us because of our wrongdoing and rebellion has turned away, and He is our salvation because "to us a child is born, to us a son is given" (Isaiah 9:6 [Hebrew verse 5]). "For God so loved the world, that he gave his only Son, that whoever believes in him should not perish but have eternal life" (John 3:16).

Why sing for joy? How could we not!

---

1. On the links between the prophecy of Immanuel in Isaiah 7:13, 14 and Isaiah 9:6, 7 [Hebrew verses 5, 6]), see Jacques B. Doukhan, *On the Way to Emmaus: Five Major Messianic Prophecies Explained* (Clarksville, MD: Lederer Books, 2012), 88, 89.

Six

Who Is Like God?
Isaiah 13, 14, 19

The many gods of the ancient Near Eastern people were part of a vast cosmic community.[1] As in human society, the relationships between these gods were hierarchical: some gods were more important, more powerful, and had wider domains than others. None of these ancient Near Eastern gods possessed exclusive power.

A God without borders
Unlike the gods of the other ancient Near Eastern people, the God of Israel—whose personal name in Hebrew is YHWH (probably pronounced something like Yahweh), which is usually translated as "the Lord"—is (not just was!) very different. He is not merely the King of the gods: He denies the divine power and authority, even the existence, of any other being who could be called "god" (Isaiah 43:10; 44:6; 45:5), and He does not permit people to acknowledge them either (Exodus 20:3).

Although YHWH was the national deity of Israel in the sense that He made a unique covenant with the Israelites (Exodus 19–24), all people on planet Earth have been subject to Him since He created the entire human race (Genesis 1; 2). Moreover, He created the entire universe, including the sun, moon, and stars (Genesis 1) and all regions of the cosmos: "Heaven and earth, the sea and the springs of water" (Revelation 14:7). He is the universal and international God, without borders (Jonah 1:9).

The book of Isaiah begins by holding God's covenant people, especially those from Judah and also from the northern kingdom of Israel, accountable to Him (Isaiah 1:1–10:4). But then He asserts His authority over the nation of Assyria (Isaiah 10:5–34). He did not hold the Assyrians responsible for keeping all the laws of His covenant with Israel, which they did not know. Rather, He judged them for their pride and brutality, which violated universal moral norms (compare Leviticus 18; Romans 1:18–32).

Isaiah 13 begins a new section of the book of Isaiah, which is indicated by a reminder of the prophet's identity—"Isaiah the son of Amoz saw" (verse 1)—and the recurrence of the term *oracle* (utterance) to introduce sections within chapters 13 through 23. These chapters pronounce judgments on the nations of the ancient Near East, with a special focus on Babylon (Isaiah 13:1–14:23).

As in the judgment against Assyria (Isaiah 10:5–34), the Lord indicts nations for offenses that they should have recognized as sins, especially those of pride (Isaiah 13:11; 16:6) and cruelty (Isaiah 14:6). However, the bulk of these prophetic oracles dramatically depict the nations' fates when they fall before divine judgments.

Isaiah's prophetic voice pounds the message home: the Judge of all the earth has arraigned all nations and has found them guilty of high crimes against Him and against humanity, for which they deserve severe punishment or destruction (compare Romans 3:23). Therefore, their condemnation is just, and they cannot escape it because the Lord is the supreme Sovereign, and even the strongest and most boasted human power is nothing to Him (Isaiah 17:13).

Even if Isaiah's oracles did not reach the Gentile nations that they addressed, their messages should have impressed on Isaiah's countrymen several points that are just as relevant for modern "new covenant" Christians. First, as part of the human race, we are no better than anyone else because we, too, have sinned. Second, if even those outside of God's covenant with limited knowledge of right principles are accountable, then we within the covenant, to whom special divine revelations have been entrusted in the inspired writings (compare Romans 3:1, 2), bear a much greater responsibility. Third, we are totally dependent on God's mercy—not help from other people (Isaiah 20:1–6)—for our survival, so our best course is to trust Him and accept the remedy for our sins that He offers (compare Romans 3:21–26). Fourth, if we have a positive relationship with Him, we do not need to fear anything or anybody because He has absolute power to take care of us (Romans 8:31–39).

So what kind of remedy does the Lord offer? Isaiah previously communicated God's free offer of pardon to His covenant people (Isaiah 1:18, 19). Now, in the midst of the judgment oracles against the nations, Isaiah 19:18–25 prophesies divine mercy and blessing for—you will not believe it unless you read it yourself—the Egyptians and the Assyrians, who had been major enemies of God's people (Isaiah 7:18), but Isaiah says they will worship Him in the future!

This remarkable prophecy, like other classical prophecies (not including the apocalyptic prophecies of Daniel and Revelation), was conditional. It would be fulfilled if the Egyptians and Assyrians would turn to the Lord. As it turns out, in later centuries, many Egyptians and Assyrians did accept the Lord and the gift of salvation through Christ's sacrifice. Today most modern Assyrians (among whom are friends of the author of this book) are Christians.

Isaiah 19 reveals God's character and intentions: He is willing to freely forgive and bless people of any nation if they accept His borderless lordship and worship Him. The fact that He can do this for Egyptians and Assyrians implies that He can also do it for others. What kind of God is this? Who is like God?

Gate of the god(s)

Isaiah's prophecies against the nations begin by pronouncing judgment on Babylon (Isaiah 13:1–14:23). This seems surprising because the greatest threat to Judah during Isaiah's ministry in the latter part of the eighth century BC and the early years of the seventh century BC was Assyria (Isaiah 7:17–20; 36:1–37:38), which dominated Babylon at that time. But divine vision reached into the future when the Neo-Babylonian king Nebuchadnezzar II would put an end to the kingdom of Judah, destroy Jerusalem and the Lord's temple, and take many of the Judahite (Jewish) people captive (2 Kings 25; 2 Chronicles 36; compare Isaiah 39:5–7) in the sixth century BC, culminating in 586 BC.

The Lord allowed Babylon to conquer Judah because His covenant nation had abandoned Him (2 Kings 24:18–25:1; 2 Chronicles 36:11–17). But just as He held Assyria—the rod of His anger against His people (Isaiah 10:5)—accountable for its pride and cruelty (verses 6–34), He also held Babylon accountable for the same sins (Isaiah 13; Daniel 4:27–33).

The Bible presents Babylon as a prime example of human pride from early times. After the Great Flood, people built the Tower of Babel—that is, Babylon (Genesis 11:1–9). In the Babylonian language, the name *Babylon* meant "Gate of the god(s)"; it was a place where humans had access to the gods. Genesis 11:9 puts a pejorative twist on the Hebrew version of the name *Babel* (*Babylon*) by deriving it from the Hebrew root *b-l-l*, which means to "mix or confuse," "because there the LORD confused the language of all the earth." Indeed, seeking access to Divinity in a wrong way results in confusion, as a myriad of false religions illustrates.

The city of Babylon went through several historical phases over many centuries, during which its political importance rose and fell. But it became and remained a dominant center of Mesopotamian culture and religion. Nebuchadnezzar II carried out a vigorous building program to make his capital of Babylon a wonder of the world, of which he was proud (Daniel 4:30). Pride was Nebuchadnezzar's downfall (verses 31–33); but he recovered from it, by God's mercy (verses 34–37).

Belshazzar, a later Neo-Babylonian ruler who coreigned with his father Nabonidus, did not learn Nebuchadnezzar's lesson. In 539 BC, he presided over Babylon's last orgy of pride. During this great supper party, he and his guests drank wine from vessels that had belonged to the Lord's temple in Jerusalem and praised their gods (Daniel 5:1–4).

No wonder Isaiah 13 is so hard on Babylon! Here the prophetic description of Babylon's fall is vivid and terrifying. It is depicted as "the day of the LORD" (verses 6, 9); it is the time for the true God to finally execute retributive justice (compare Jeremiah 46:10; Amos 5:18–20; Zephaniah 1:7, 14). "And Babylon, the glory of kingdoms" "will never be inhabited or lived in for all generations" (Isaiah 13:19, 20).

Indeed, Belshazzar's supper was his last because the Medo-Persian army of Cyrus captured Babylon that night, and Belshazzar was killed (Daniel 5:30). Cyrus took the city without a battle, so the city remained unharmed but lost its independence forever. Babylon declined over several centuries and was progressively abandoned so that the Roman emperor Septimius Severus found the city completely deserted in AD 199.[2]

Why wasn't Babylon suddenly destroyed, as portrayed in Isaiah 13? Perhaps because the prophecy was conditional, as was Jonah's prophecy regarding the destruction of Nineveh, and God mercifully gave the Babylonians more time. Also, Isaiah 13 may compact into a single event the long process of Babylon's demise from its capture by Cyrus to its eventual abandonment.

References to "the Medes" attacking Babylon (Isaiah 13:17) and "the Chaldeans" owning Babylon (verse 19) ensure that the Medo-Persian conquest is at least partly in view. However, verse 11 points beyond the events of 539 BC: "I will punish the world for its evil." Babylon represents human pride and rebellion against the Lord, which He will ultimately obliterate when Christ comes again to conquer planet Earth (Revelation 19:11–21). Shortly before this cataclysmic event, the proud, immoral, and persecuting religious power that the book of Revelation calls "Babylon the Great" (Revelation 16:19; 17:5; 18:2, 21) will suddenly collapse (Revelation 16–18).

Christ is the only legitimate Gate of God. He is the only means by which human beings have access to God. As Jesus said to Nathanael, "Truly, truly, I say to you, you will see heaven opened, and the angels of God ascending and descending on the Son of Man" (John 1:51). By this, Jesus identified Himself with the ladder that Jacob saw in a dream, which went from Earth to heaven, and angels ascended and descended on it (Genesis 28:12). When Jacob awoke, he declared, "This is none other than the house of God, and this is the gate of heaven" (verse 17). So he named the place *Bethel*, which means "the house of God" (verse 19). Here, not at Babylon, was the true Gate of God.

"Day Star, son of Dawn" versus Michael

The fall of Babylon in 539 BC was good for the Jews because Cyrus, the Persian king, set them free to return to their homeland soon afterward (2 Chronicles 36:22, 23; Ezra 1). Isaiah 14:1 looks forward to this return. Verses 4 through 21 prophesy a proverbial speech that the people of the Lord direct against "the king of Babylon" (verse 4) to celebrate their liberation by God from this king's ruthless oppression. In a truly grim word picture, the once mighty and glorious monarch is brought down to Sheol, the place of the dead, with a bed of maggots and worms as his covers (verse 11).

The next verses are astonishing:

"How you are fallen from heaven,
    O Day Star, son of Dawn!
How you are cut down to the ground,

you who laid the nations low!
You said in your heart,
  'I will ascend to heaven;
above the stars of God
  I will set my throne on high;
I will sit on the mount of assembly
  in the far reaches of the north;
I will ascend above the heights of the clouds;
  I will make myself like the Most High' " (verses 12–14).

No king of the Neo-Babylonian Empire ever said this or would even dare to think it. Even arrogant Belshazzar praised his gods (Daniel 5:4); he did not attempt to replace a minor deity, let alone the most high, heavenly God.

It seems clear that these words go beyond a human king of ancient Babylon, just as Isaiah 13:11 points beyond the fall of this city in 539 BC to a global event. But who would dare to contemplate replacing the Lord Himself? Revelation 12 identifies someone who warred against God's heavenly forces in an attempt to take control: "The great dragon . . . that ancient serpent" who fought against "Michael and his angels" in heaven, "but he was defeated" and cast down to Earth (verses 7–9). The dragon is "the devil and Satan, the deceiver of the whole world" (verse 9). He had been so magnificent that he was called "Day Star, son of Dawn" (Isaiah 14:12; "Day Star" equates with "Lucifer" in the KJV and NKJV, following the Latin Vulgate).[3] But his proud ambition to ascend above the clouds to the position of the Most High, which has led to his cruel reign of terror over the earth—including through the human kings of Babylon—will bring him down to Sheol, which is the place of the dead (Isaiah 14:15–17).

Isaiah's message contains warning and hope for the Lord's people of all eras. The warning is that pride does come before a fall (see Proverbs 16:18). Satan tempts us to be proud like him, supposing that we are our own masters who are in charge of our destinies. But God promises to bring down such arrogance with a mighty crash.

The divinely assured hope is that the Lord will end the oppressive power of satanic evil (compare Isaiah 27:1: "the fleeing serpent . . . the dragon that is in the sea"), with its vicious demonic (formerly angelic) and human agents. Reinforcing this hope, Isaiah 24–27 goes on to prophesy of God's conquest of the earth, resulting in its desolation (Isaiah 24) and the punishment of "the kings of the earth" (verse 21). God's people will welcome Him, exclaiming, "Behold, this is our God; we have waited for him, that he might save us. This is the LORD; we have waited for him; let us be glad and rejoice in his salvation" (Isaiah 25:9). At that time, "He will swallow up death forever; and the LORD GOD will wipe away tears from all faces" (verse 8; compare Revelation 21:4).

According to Daniel 12, the rise of "Michael, the great prince who has charge of your people" (verse 1), will lead to the deliverance of God's loyal people. It was Michael, the Commander of God's army of angels, who defeated Satan in heaven (Revelation 12), and Michael will defeat him on Earth. Satan wanted to be like God (Isaiah 14:14), but Michael's name means "Who is like God?" This can be understood as a rhetorical question. The answer is, Nobody but God Himself!

---

1. See, for example, Karel van der Toorn, Bob Becking, and Pieter W. van der Horst, eds., *Dictionary of Deities and Demons in the Bible*, 2nd rev. ed. (Grand Rapids, MI: Eerdmans, 1999).

2. Georges Roux, *Ancient Iraq*, 2nd ed. (London, UK: Penguin Books, 1980), 357, 358, 377, 378, 389.

3. For a detailed analysis of Isaiah 14:12–15 and the parallel passage in Ezekiel 28:12–19, leading to the conclusion that they describe the fall of Satan, see José M. Bertoluci, "The Son of the Morning and the Guardian Cherub in the Context of the Controversy Between Good and Evil" (ThD diss., Andrews University, 1985), https://digitalcommons.andrews.edu/cgi/viewcontent.cgi?article=1016&context=dissertations.

Seven

What Gives You Courage?
Isaiah 36-39

The events described in Isaiah 36 and 37 are some of the most dramatic in the entire Bible. They are also among the best attested to in biblical history, with a wealth of information coming from many sources, including the parallel accounts in 2 Kings 18; 19 and 2 Chronicles 32, ancient Near Eastern texts, Assyrian art, and archaeology. In the midst of all the fascinating historical details in these chapters is a striking illustration that encapsulates the message of the book of Isaiah. It takes place in a life of fervent faith that is rewarded by a stunning divine intervention at a time of terrifying crisis, when all earthly factors point to the imminent obliteration of God's remnant people.

Enemies telling the same story

Isaiah 36 begins, "In the fourteenth year of King Hezekiah, Sennacherib king of Assyria came up against all the fortified cities of Judah and took them. And the king of Assyria sent the Rabshakeh from Lachish to King Hezekiah at Jerusalem, with a great army" (verses 1, 2). Sennacherib's own annals (written by his scribes in cuneiform on clay prisms) of his third military campaign describe his exploits in more detail from his perspective as Hezekiah's enemy:

> As for Hezekiah, the Judean, I besieged forty-six of his fortified walled cities and surrounding smaller towns, which were without number. Using packed-down ramps and applying battering rams, infantry attacks by mines, breeches [*sic* breaches], and siege machines, I conquered (them). I took out 200,150 people, young and old, male and female, horses, mules, donkeys, camels, cattle, and sheep, without number, and counted them as spoil. He himself, I locked up within Jerusalem, his royal city, like a bird in a cage. I surrounded him with earthworks, and made it unthinkable for him to exit by the city gate. His cities which I had despoiled I cut off from his land and gave them to Mitinti, king of Ashdod, Padi, king of Ekron and Ṣilli-bel, king of Gaza, and thus diminished his land. I imposed dues and gifts for my lordship upon him, in addition to the former tribute, their yearly payment.[1]

To the extent that enemies agree on what happened during a conflict between them, we can be quite certain that they are telling the truth. The Bible and Sennacherib's annals agree on several aspects of the story, including the fact that the Assyrians first conquered most of Judah. Soon after, the Assyrian army came to Jerusalem and threatened it. Also, the Assyrian annals indicate that Sennacherib imposed payments on Hezekiah, and 2 Kings 18:14–16 reports one payment that Hezekiah offered him.

However, there is no biblical parallel for the continuation of the story in Sennacherib's annals, which served as propaganda: "He, Hezekiah, was overwhelmed by the awesome splendor of my lordship." What follows is a list of the various kinds of gifts that Hezekiah allegedly sent to Sennacherib.[2] Thus the annals claimed victory, which they defined as success in forcing Hezekiah to submit to Assyrian rule. But according to the Bible, Sennacherib's invasion ended very differently.

Faith, courage, and deliverance

Now for the story behind the story. King Ahaz of Judah had bribed the Assyrian king Tiglath-pileser III to save him from the Syrian–northern Israelite alliance (2 Kings 16:7–9). Hezekiah, Ahaz's son, inherited his father's onerous obligation to Assyria, which was ruled after Tiglath-pileser by Shalmaneser V and then Sargon II. Unlike his father, Hezekiah wholeheartedly followed the Lord and carried out a major religious reform by destroying places and objects of idolatry, restoring the temple and the worship there, and reinstituting the Festival of Passover (2 Kings 18:1–6; 2 Chronicles 29–31). "He trusted in the LORD, the God of Israel" (2 Kings 18:5), and with such faith comes divine blessing and courage: "And the LORD was with him; wherever he went out, he prospered. He rebelled against the king of Assyria and would not serve him" (verse 7). Hezekiah did not believe that it was God's will for His people to be subject to Assyria.

Hezekiah saw an opportunity for freedom at a moment of apparent Assyrian vulnerability when Sargon II was killed in 705 BC during a military campaign. Hezekiah conspired with some nations in his region to rebel against Assyria, signified by withholding tribute. Nations in the eastern part of the Assyrian Empire also rebelled at this time. But the rebels had underestimated Sargon's son Sennacherib, who rapidly consolidated his power and quelled the revolts in the east by means of his first two military campaigns. Then he turned to the west and threw the brutal might of the Assyrian army against Hezekiah and those allied with him.

This is when Sennacherib took Hezekiah's fortified cities and "intended to fight against Jerusalem" (2 Chronicles 32:2).

Hezekiah's attempt to save himself and Jerusalem by apologizing to Sennacherib for his rebellion and paying off the Assyrian king was unsuccessful (2 Kings 18:14–17). So Hezekiah prepared Jerusalem for an inevitable siege (2 Chronicles 32:3–6) and encouraged his people by telling them: "Be strong and courageous. Do not be afraid or dismayed before the king of Assyria and all the horde that is with him, for there are more with us than with him. With him is an arm of flesh, but with us is the LORD our God, to help us and to fight our battles" (verses 7, 8).

Hezekiah knew that in worldly terms, he and Jerusalem were doomed. During this period, the Assyrians were not losing battles, and when they besieged a city, they conquered it. They killed anyone who rebelled against them, especially the ringleaders of the revolts, as Hezekiah was.

If the Assyrians succeeded in taking Jerusalem and deporting and scattering its inhabitants, as they had done to the people of Samaria, which was the capital of northern Israel (2 Kings 18:11), the Judahite people would cease to be a nation and would suffer the fate of the northern Israelites who lost their identity and were absorbed into the populations of the nations to which they were taken. If that happened, the Lord would no longer have a remnant people on the face of the whole earth to represent Him. The stakes were high in the great controversy between God and Satan! While the Babylonians later deported many Judahites to Babylon (2 Kings 25:11; 2 Chronicles 36:20), the Babylonians generally allowed them to remain together and keep their identity, unlike the Assyrians.

But why should the Assyrians go to all the trouble of taking Jerusalem by siege warfare if they could intimidate Hezekiah and his people into simply surrendering? Thus Sennacherib sent his *rabshakeh* (literally, "chief cupbearer"; compare Nehemiah 1:11), a high-ranking official, to Jerusalem to persuade Hezekiah and the inhabitants of Jerusalem to give up. Ironically, the rabshakeh came to the same place outside the wall of Jerusalem where Isaiah had met Ahaz years before when urging him not to get involved with Assyria: "the conduit of the upper pool on the highway to the Washer's Field" (Isaiah 36:2; compare Isaiah 7:3). There he delivered his message to three of Hezekiah's top officials (Isaiah 36:3), but he spoke loudly enough that he could be heard by the Jerusalemites sitting on the wall (verses 11, 12).

The rabshakeh's speech was brilliant (verses 4–20). He understood that Hezekiah's resistance to surrendering was based on his belief that Jerusalem possibly could survive an Assyrian siege. So speaking for Sennacherib, he sought to undermine that trust and turn the people of Jerusalem against Hezekiah by beginning with an overall rhetorical question to Hezekiah: "On what do you rest this trust of yours?" (verse 4). The gods of other nations had not saved them from Assyria, so why should the Judahites believe Hezekiah when he said that the Lord would deliver them (verses 18–20)? Thus the rabshakeh and his master Sennacherib directly challenged the Living God and mocked His ability to free the Judahite prey from the Assyrian predator (Isaiah 37:4, 17; compare Exodus 5:2).

The rabshakeh's speech was devastating to Hezekiah and his officials (Isaiah 36:22–37:1). This test of faith was even more severe than that which Ahaz had faced (compare Isaiah 7:9b). However, rather than caving in to despair, Hezekiah did what every person of faith does during a time of crisis: he did not attempt to fix the situation by himself, as Ahaz did, but looked up to God. The king "went into the house of the LORD" (Isaiah 37:1) and contacted the prophet Isaiah (verses 2–4).

Isaiah's response from the Lord was brief and to the point: the Assyrian king would "hear a rumor and return to his own land, and I will make him fall by the sword in his own land" (verse 7). Sure enough, Sennacherib's plan to take Jerusalem was interrupted when he heard that Tirhakah, the king of Cush, was coming to fight him (verse 9). But before taking his army away, he sent a threatening message to King Hezekiah, indicating that he would be back (verses 10–13).

That was bad news! Again, Hezekiah took it to God. In fact, he went to the temple and spread out the letter before the Lord (verse 14). He prayed, addressing God as "LORD of hosts, God of Israel, enthroned above the cherubim, you are the God, you alone, of all the kingdoms of the earth; you have made heaven and earth" (verse 16). Hezekiah acknowledged that the Assyrians had destroyed other nations with their idol gods (verses 18, 19), but he pled with God: "So now, O LORD our God, save us from his hand, that all the kingdoms of the earth may know that you alone are the LORD" (verse 20).

Hezekiah understood a profound truth. This was not just about saving his people and himself from a grim earthly fate with temporary consequences. More than that, the most important thing was God's reputation in the world (compare Exodus 32:12; Numbers 14:13–16; Ezekiel 36:22–36; 37:28), by which He draws people to Himself for their eternal well-being. The Lord promised that Judah and Jerusalem would survive and thrive again and that the Assyrian king would not succeed in entering Jerusalem or even besieging it. Rather, he would just go home because God would defend the city for His own sake and that of his servant David (Isaiah 37:30–35).

The Bible and ancient history, including archaeology, agree that Sennacherib did not conquer Jerusalem and that the city, with the rest of Judah, did recover from his invasion. Even Sennacherib's annals do not claim that he took Jerusalem or captured Hezekiah. The pictures on the walls of his palace only celebrate his triumph over nearby Lachish, which was a much smaller prize.

These events are very strange. During this period, at the height of the Neo-Assyrian Empire, the Assyrian superpower military machine accomplished whatever it set out to do. Scholars who do not believe in miraculous divine interventions are puzzled because they cannot explain what happened to prevent what was otherwise inevitable.

The Bible provides the explanation immediately after Isaiah's speech: "And the angel of the LORD went out and struck down 185,000 in the camp of the Assyrians. And when people arose early in the morning, behold, these were all dead bodies" (Isaiah 37:36; see also 2 Kings 19:35; 2 Chronicles 32:21). There was nothing Sennacherib could do but go home to Nineveh, where, according to the Bible, he was later assassinated by two of his sons while he was worshiping in the temple of his god (Isaiah 37:37, 38; 2 Kings 19:37; 2 Chronicles 32:21). Ironically, while Hezekiah received help from the Lord at His temple (mentioned above), Sennacherib met his demise at the house of his false god.

Missed opportunity

As if Hezekiah didn't have enough to deal with during the stressful time when Sennacherib was out to get him, he became very ill, and Isaiah affirmed that he would die (Isaiah 38:1, 21; 2 Kings 20:1). But Hezekiah did not want to die; his death would deprive Judah of his leadership and make his nation vulnerable during the transition of power. So he prayed and wept (Isaiah 38:2, 3; 2 Kings 20:2, 3).

God responded through Isaiah, promising to heal the king so that on the third day he would be able to go up to the temple (2 Kings 20:4, 5) to worship and praise the Lord. Moreover, the Lord would give Hezekiah an additional fifteen years of life and would deliver him and Jerusalem from the Assyrian king (Isaiah 38:4–6; 2 Kings 20:6). As a remedy, Isaiah directed that a poultice of figs should be applied to the boil, which was one of the symptoms of Hezekiah's disease (Isaiah 38:21). Whether or not the poultice had any medicinal value, its prescription by the Divine Physician and its effectiveness were interventions from God.

Hezekiah believed God's promise but asked for confirmation through a sign (Isaiah 38:22; 2 Kings 20:8; compare Judges

6:36–40). According to 2 Kings 20, which gives a slightly fuller account than Isaiah 38, Isaiah gave the king a choice: Should the shadow on a sundial go forward or back ten steps? Hezekiah chose the latter, and God answered Isaiah's request that this happen (verses 9–11; compare Isaiah 38:7, 8). Ironically, this sign showed itself on the sundial of Ahaz (2 Kings 20:11; Isaiah 38:8)—the king without faith who had rejected a sign from the Lord (Isaiah 7:11, 12).

Now let us attempt to put this in perspective. To change the time on your watch, you can turn a small dial or push a button or two. But how do you change the time on a sundial? That requires a readjustment of our solar system, which God alone can do. He halted the movement of the earth in relation to the sun and moon so Joshua could finish a battle (Joshua 10:12–14), and now He halted the movement of the earth in relation to the sun to give one man confirmation that he would be healed, keep living, and be delivered from his enemies! The Lord had offered to give Ahaz a sign of deliverance that was "deep as Sheol or high as heaven" (Isaiah 7:11), and now He gave Hezekiah, Ahaz's son, a sign that was "high as heaven." That is how important human faith is to God!

You can change the time on your watch without anyone noticing because it does not affect anyone else, but altering the relative position of the sun and the earth affects everyone in the world. Hezekiah's sign could not escape the notice of the Babylonians, who meticulously tracked the movements of heavenly bodies in order to discern omens that they thought would indicate future events. They kept careful records and made detailed star charts on clay tablets, which modern astronomers have verified as accurate. Imagine their surprise when the sun went back ten degrees! What kind of omen was this?

The omen was so stupendous that the Babylonians were compelled to seek its cause and significance. It appears that they managed to trace it to Hezekiah's recovery. Therefore, "at that time Merodach-baladan the son of Baladan, king of Babylon, sent envoys with letters and a present to Hezekiah, for he heard that he had been sick and had recovered" (Isaiah 39:1; see also 2 Kings 20:12).

Why would a Mesopotamian king send envoys hundreds of miles away to distant Judah just to congratulate its king on his recovery from illness? Obviously, there was more to it than that, which correlates with what we know about Merodach-baladan, a Chaldean whose Babylonian name was Marduk-apla-iddina. Like Hezekiah, he was rebelling against Assyria. No doubt, the Babylonian king was reaching out to Hezekiah as a potentially valuable ally. If Hezekiah was empowered by a Deity who could heal him and even alter the position of the sun, what could He do to Assyria!

Hezekiah was flattered by the arrival of the Babylonian envoys and the message from their king, and to demonstrate how great he was, he graciously gave them a grand show-and-tell tour of all of his wealth (Isaiah 39:2; 2 Kings 20:13). The king of Judah forgot to focus on impressing the Babylonians with the greatness of his God, who had healed him and given him an amazing sign.

Unfortunately, Hezekiah was not the last to miss an opportunity to give glory and praise to God, to whom we owe everything. If we are going to brag, we should brag about God or "boast in the Lord" (Psalm 34:2 [Hebrew verse 3]; see also 1 Corinthians 1:31; 2 Corinthians 10:17). Praising Him by sharing our testimony of the great things He has done for us is the most effective form of evangelistic communication (compare Mark 5:19, 20).

As it turned out, Hezekiah's mistake would have far-reaching consequences. The Babylonians remembered that there were riches in Judah, and later they came back with an army to get them. Through Isaiah, the Lord informed Hezekiah that all of his possessions and some of his sons would be taken away to

Babylon (Isaiah 39:5–7; 2 Kings 20:16–18). So, even as early as this, Babylonian captivity was inevitable, although it could have been limited to the deportation of just a few people. This reference to the Babylonian deportation explains why chapters 38 and 39 are placed in this location in the book of Isaiah, rather than before chapters 36 and 37, which recount events that happened a little later. Chapters 38 and 39 serve as a transition to chapters 40 and following, which concern the future Babylonian exile.

The narratives of Isaiah 36–39 refer to several things from which a person could gain courage: force of arms, protective walls, material possessions, alliances with other people, and faith in the Living God. What gives you courage?

---

1. Mordechai Cogan, trans., "Sennacherib's Siege of Jerusalem," in *The Context of Scripture*, ed. William W. Hallo, vol. 2 (Leiden: Brill, 1997), 303.

2. Cogan, 303.

Eight

Is Your Hard Labor Over?
Isaiah 40

World War II officially ended in Europe on May 7, 1945. Britain's Ministry of Information announced that the next day, Tuesday, May 8, would be a public holiday called Victory in Europe Day, which has come to be known as V-E Day.[1] After years of "blood, toil, tears and sweat,"[2] pent-up emotions exploded in rejoicing. Millions of people turned out to celebrate in the streets of Great Britain, where tens of thousands in London filled Trafalgar Square and along the Mall to Buckingham Palace.

It is over!
Isaiah 40 celebrates the end of another period of suffering:

> Comfort, comfort my people, says your God.
> Speak tenderly to Jerusalem,
>   and cry to her
> that her warfare is ended,
>   that her iniquity is pardoned,
> that she has received from the Lord's hand
>   double for all her sins (verses 1, 2).

It is over!

The Hebrew word translated as "warfare" in these verses can refer to a host—that is, a large group, such as an army; war, battle, or military service; or hard compulsory labor that one is forced to do (Job 7:1; 10:17; 14:14). This last idea seems to be the one in view in Isaiah 40:2: the forced labor is fulfilled, meaning that its time is up.

Is God unjust in giving the people of Jerusalem double punishment for their sins? No; in Old Testament law, justice required that those who committed theft must pay double to include both restitution and a penalty for wrongdoing (Exodus 22:4, 7, 9 [Hebrew verses 3, 6, 8]). If a thief could not pay because he had nothing, "he shall be sold for his theft" (verse 3 [Hebrew verse 2]); in other words, he must pay off his debt with forced labor. Jerusalem's sin was far more serious than theft: She had committed murder and idolatry and had broken the Lord's covenant, for which she richly deserved death. But God had mercifully sentenced her to mere double payment, as though she had merely stolen something. She did not have the means to pay, so He made her work off the debt with forced labor.

What kind of forced labor was Jerusalem obligated to perform? Isaiah 40 does not say, but the concept that the whole royal capital city of Judah would be subjected to this humiliating service for a period of time implies that the labor was imposed by a foreign power who conquered the city (compare Deuteronomy 20:11). This power was not Assyria, which did not succeed in conquering Jerusalem (Isaiah 36, 37), and the book of Isaiah only mentions Assyria once again (Isaiah 52:4) in the context of past history.

Isaiah 39 gives a clue regarding the foreign oppressor's identity: Some princes of Judah would be taken to Babylon, where they would serve as eunuchs in the palace of the king of Babylon (verse 7). Earlier in the book, the message of judgment on Babylon includes a promise that "the LORD will have compassion on Jacob . . . and will set them in their own land" (Isaiah 14:1). This implies that the Babylonians will have exiled them, and the next verse mentions "those who oppressed them" (verse 2). The following verse is a striking parallel to Isaiah 40:2 because it refers to the Lord giving His people "rest" from their "pain and turmoil and the hard service" with which they "were made to serve" (Isaiah 14:3).

The beginning of Isaiah 40 sets the stage for the following chapters, culminating in chapter 66. This final section of the book largely focuses on the consolation and restoration of the Lord's people following their exile. The consolation is expressed in exquisite and profound poetic oratory that is virtually peerless in human literature. The restoration theme contrasts with the book's earlier emphasis on judgment against God's people. Its literary style features the repetition of words for emphasis (for example, Isaiah 40:1), parallelism (for example, verses 3, 4), rhetorical questions (for example, verses 12–14), many assonances and alliterations (for example, verses 3, 4, 6, 9–12), and an abundance of vivid metaphors and word pictures (for example, verses 3, 4, 6–11). The marvelous literary quality serves as a fitting vehicle to convey the soaring concepts from the mind and heart of God.

Pictures of deliverance

As in the music of Ludwig van Beethoven, the oratory of Isaiah is full of dramatic shifts that grip one's attention and compel the listener to concentrate on understanding how the parts fit together into a cohesive masterpiece. Following the introductory proclamation in Isaiah 40:1, 2 ("cry to her"), three scenes portraying different aspects of the theme of comfort following punishment are described. Each scene is introduced by or includes a proclamation: verse 3: "A voice cries"; verse 6: "A voice says, 'Cry!' "; verse 9: "Lift up your voice."

The first scene (verses 3–5) begins as follows: "A voice cries:

'In the wilderness prepare the way of the LORD; make straight in the desert a highway for our God' " (verse 3). Interestingly, the parallelism between preparing the way in the wilderness and making a highway straight in the desert clearly shows that the punctuation in the English Standard Version is correct, rather than the New King James Version's "The voice of one crying in the wilderness: 'Prepare the way of the LORD.' " The picture is one of preparing for the Divine King to travel across the ground toward His people to reveal His glory (verse 5). God's glory represents His divine presence and power, including the power to protect His people (compare Isaiah 58:8) and liberate them from oppression and forced labor.

The scenario of road preparation is metaphorical, but what does it represent? Receiving the Lord's glorious presence requires purity, so there must be a preparation of purification to meet Him (Isaiah 4:3–5; compare Exodus 19:10, 11, 15; 30:17–21; Leviticus 7:20, 21; 16:4). In Isaiah 4, "the filth of the daughters of Zion" and "the bloodstains of Jerusalem" (verse 4) that must be washed away refer to moral faults (Isaiah 2, 3). The Lord purges these sins, but the remnant who remain in Jerusalem and are called "holy" (Isaiah 4:3) will have prepared for Him by loyally cooperating with Him in their lives.

Later in the Bible, Malachi predicted that the Lord's way would be prepared by a special messenger (Malachi 3:1). Jesus explained that this was John the Baptist (Matthew 11:10). Matthew 3:3 also applies the prophecy of Isaiah 40:3 to John the Baptist:

For this is he who was spoken of by the prophet Isaiah when he said,

"The voice of one crying in the wilderness:
'Prepare the way of the Lord;
   make his paths straight.' "

This punctuation makes sense in this context because John was "preaching in the wilderness of Judea" [verse 1].

Malachi 4:5, 6 (Hebrew verses 3:23, 24) predicts another messenger, called "Elijah the prophet," to prepare the way of the Lord "before the great and awesome day of the Lord comes. And he will turn the hearts of fathers to their children and the hearts of children to their fathers." Jesus applied this to John the Baptist (Matthew 11:14; 17:11–13; Mark 9:12, 13), but there must be a further fulfillment just before the second coming of Christ on "the great and awesome day of the Lord."

Indeed, Revelation 14:6–12 predicted that three angels would prepare the way of the Lord's coming by delivering gospel messages that appeal to all the inhabitants of planet Earth to worship only the Creator and encourage God's people to "keep the commandments of God and the faith of Jesus" (verse 12, NKJV). The commandments of God are based on love (Matthew 22:37–40) and so is the faith of Jesus (for example, Galatians 2:20). In this, the concepts of Revelation 14:12 are like the Elijah message of relational reconciliation (Malachi 4:5, 6), which is also based on love and is placed alongside a reminder to keep God's commandments (verse 4). Jesus commissioned His followers to proclaim His gospel (Matthew 24:14; 28:19, 20). So we, His end-time people, are Elijah and the three angels, to whom God has entrusted the awesome privilege and responsibility of preparing the way of the Lord.

Isaiah ministered during the last years of King Uzziah, who died in 740 BC, through the reign of Hezekiah (see Isaiah 1:1) and probably to the beginning of the reign of Manasseh in the 680s BC. The Babylonian exile ended in the 530s BC— nearly a century and a half after Isaiah's time. Why would Isaiah address events so far in the future, ministering to generations yet unborn? Such prophecies prove a major point, which is highly relevant to us as the Lord's end-time people: the true God is unique in that He knows the future (Isaiah 41:21–29; 42:9; 46:9–11; see further in chapter 9 of this book). Therefore, He has the wisdom to guide His people into the future, and His promises to us will surely be fulfilled. So even though we may go through hard times, we should not despair because He will be with us and bring us through to the other side (Psalm 23:4–6). This kind of hope, provided by the divine messages of Isaiah, Jeremiah, and Ezekiel, sustained a remnant of the Babylonian exiles so that they did not give up on the Lord.

We have found that the prophecies of Isaiah were to guide God's people in ancient times. But they also contain principles that reverberate through salvation history until the present.

The second scene in Isaiah 40 pictures all beings of flesh as grass or wildflowers that wither and fade "when the breath of the LORD blows" on them, "but the word of our God will stand forever" (verses 7, 8; compare Psalm 103:15–18). This passage emphasizes the transience of human life and our vulnerability to divine power, in radical contrast with God's eternal word. He not only can make us wither by blowing punishment upon us (compare Isaiah 40:23, 24) but also is totally capable of restoring us. He is compassionate and tender toward us, remembering that we are dust (Psalm 103:13, 14), and His love is everlasting (verse 17).

The third scene in Isaiah 40 is related to the first scene in that the Lord is coming. Here Zion, or Jerusalem, is personi-fied as a female (feminine gender in Hebrew) reporter or news announcer. She is told to ascend a high mountain and shout to the other cities of Judah the good news that their God is coming with powerful force for their benefit and He will "tend his flock like a shepherd" (verse 11). In Bible times a mountain was a strategic place from which to make oneself heard before the invention of loudspeakers (Judges 9:7). Here, the good news of God's favor is declared for all to hear. He will take care of His people as a shepherd provides for his sheep (compare Psalm 23).

Once Jerusalem has the assurance of deliverance, the message must go out to the rest of the country that divine help is on the way, and their troubles are now history. Not only is God mighty to save, but He is considerate and tender in the way He leads. A king is the shepherd of his people (compare 2 Samuel 5:2), and the Lord is the ultimate Good Shepherd (compare Matthew 2:6; John 10:11–16).

The incomparable greatness of God

Lest anyone doubt the Lord's ability to take care of His people, the rest of Isaiah 40 puts His greatness into perspective (verses 12–31). First, a series of rhetorical questions drive home the point that His knowledge is vast and underived from any other source (verses 12–14). Nations are tiny in comparison with Him; they are "like a drop from a bucket" (verse 15) and "are as nothing before him" (verse 17), and their "inhabitants are like grasshoppers" (verse 22).

Therefore, "to whom then will you liken God, or what likeness compare with him?" (verse 18). The obviously correct rhetorical answer is: nobody and nothing. This question simultaneously concludes the previous verses and introduces the following ones that refute the wrong answer: an idol that is set up so it cannot even move (verses 19, 20). For evidence of God's incomparability, just look up at the stars. He is the Creator of everything (verse 26). As the Eternal Creator who never tires, He gives strength to those who wait for Him to help them (verses 28–31).

"Comfort, comfort my people, says your God" (Isaiah 40:1). Have you accepted and embraced His powerful and tender comfort as a gift? Is your hard labor over?

1. Gerald D. Swick, "V-E Day 1945: The Celebration Heard 'Round the World," Military Times, May 8, 2019, https://www.militarytimes.com/off-duty/military-culture/2019/05/08/v-e-day-1945-the-celebration-heard-round-the-world/.

2. Winston Churchill, "Blood, Toil, Tears and Sweat," speech to House of Commons, May 13, 1940, International Churchill Society, transcript and audio recording, 3:28, https://winstonchurchill.org/resources/speeches/1940-the-finest-hour/blood-toil-tears-and-sweat-2/.

Nine

What Is Your Future?
Isaiah 41, 42, 44, 45

Wouldn't it be helpful to know what will happen in the future? The book of Isaiah claims that God knows the future and that this unique ability is powerful proof that He is the true God (Isaiah 41:4, 21–23, 26, 27). His revelations of the future to human beings are selective: He reveals enough for us to trust in Him as the true God, understand His work of saving us, and cooperate with Him by loyally following His instructions (Deuteronomy 29:29). Humans do not always understand God's predictions before they are fulfilled, but He gives them so that when the events do take place, people may believe in Him (John 14:29).

Isaiah's most striking evidence that the Lord knows the future is his prediction that Cyrus would defeat the oppressors of his people and deliver them. Isaiah 44:28–45:7, 13 are stunningly specific verses, speaking of the actions of God:

"Who says of Cyrus, 'He is my shepherd,
    and he shall fulfill all my purpose';
saying of Jerusalem, 'She shall be built,'
    and of the temple, 'Your foundation shall be laid.' "

Thus says the LORD to his anointed, to Cyrus,
    whose right hand I have grasped . . . (Isaiah 44:28–45:1).

These verses can only speak of Cyrus the Persian, who came from the east and the north of Babylon to conquer it in 539 BC. That event happened nearly a century and a half after the death of Isaiah in the 680s BC!

After Cyrus took over Babylon, he fulfilled Isaiah's prediction by releasing the exiled Jews so that they could return to their homeland and rebuild the temple in Jerusalem (2 Chronicles 36:22, 23; Ezra 1:1–4). Thus, Cyrus began the process of restoring the temple, which the Lord Himself had decreed: "They finished their building by decree of the God of Israel and by decree of Cyrus and Darius and Artaxerxes king of Persia" (Ezra 6:14). Does God know the future?

Objections to God's foreknowledge

Historical-critical scholars reject the idea that Isaiah of Jerusalem predicted Cyrus by name nearly a century and a half before the Persian king conquered Babylon; they do not believe that such predictions or other interventions by God, such as miracles, are possible. Instead, they theorize that a later unnamed person living during the time of Cyrus, a so-called second Isaiah, must have written the portion of the book of Isaiah that contains this "prediction"—history presented as prediction— and other elements that especially relate to a setting in the Babylonian exile. This section consists of Isaiah 40–66 or 40–55 if, as many scholars maintain, there was a third author who wrote chapters 56–66 during the time of the restoration after the Exile. However, there is no solid evidence that anyone but Isaiah of Jerusalem was the human author of the book that bears his name.

Some theologians object to the idea that God knows all of the future because this seems to cause two problems. First, if

He already knows what decisions human beings will make, doesn't this override human free will so that the fates of all are predestined because our choices are irrelevant? No, the entire Bible repeatedly and emphatically affirms that human choices are crucial (for example, Genesis 4:7; Deuteronomy 30:15–20; Joshua 24:15; Revelation 3:20; 14:6–12). We decide whether we will be saved or lost by choosing whether or not to accept God's free salvation by faith in Christ and His sacrifice (Romans 3:21–26; 6:23). It is like when Noah and his family boarded the ark: God did not force anyone on or off the ark but accepted the choices that people made (Genesis 7).

The fact that God knows the choices that we will make does not mean that He determines those choices. To imperfectly illustrate the difference between foreknowledge and free will, if you know (although not with the certainty that God knows) that your children will accept your offer to take them for a day out to a zoo or aquarium, are you forcing them to go? Of course not!

The second alleged problem with God's absolute foreknowledge is an issue of *theodicy*, which refers to the justification of His character. If God's character truly is love, as the Bible explicitly states (Exodus 34:6, 7; 1 John 4:8, 16), why wouldn't He prevent suffering if He knows in advance what is going to happen?

Denying divine foreknowledge does not solve the theodicy problem because it fails to address the question of why God does not stop suffering in progress, which He could see even if He could not predict the future. For example, even if God did not know in advance what the Nazis would do at Auschwitz, why didn't He intervene while an estimated 1.1 million people, mostly Jews, were being murdered at that concentration camp?

The Bible explains that suffering and death resulted from bad choices by God's created beings, including human beings (Genesis 3; Romans 6:23); they were products of the great cosmic battle between divine love (including both justice and mercy) and rebellious selfishness. God did not want or cause the conflict, but He permitted it and its consequences because He created beings, including human beings, with free choice so that they can have the potential to love Him and each other. Love is impossible without free will; it cannot be forced. But free will carries risk: the ability to choose God is also the ability to choose against Him.

God will ultimately put a complete end to all selfishness, suffering, and death (Revelation 20–22). Love will win in the end. But in the meantime, God does not use His foreknowledge and power to prevent or stop all suffering, although He gives windows of hope through miracles of healing and protection. He provides opportunities for people to make intelligent choices by letting them see the contrast between His love and the cruel regime of sin and Satan—the rebellious ruler of this world (John 12:31).

Human beings do not understand how God can see far into the future, "declaring the end from the beginning and from ancient times things not yet done" (Isaiah 46:10); it is an ability that defies science as we know it. But the Bible gives us plenty of evidence to support God's claim, including the fulfilled predictions of Cyrus and the timing of the Messiah's coming (Daniel 9:24–27; compare Luke 3:1).[1] Especially impressive are the almost completely fulfilled prophecies of Daniel 2, 7, 8, 11, and 12, which cover not just centuries but millennia.

God's unique foreknowledge has four important implications. First, we have hope for the future because we can rest assured that the Lord is the only true God, the sovereign Creator, who can save us (Isaiah 44:1–45:7; 46:3–13; 48:3–21).

Second, God can providentially work out His will on our behalf with wisdom and effectiveness. He does not force human decisions but works with and in spite of them (Genesis 50:20; Romans 8:28).

Third, when a true messenger from the Lord makes a prediction in His name, the prediction comes true (Isaiah 44:26). This is a test of a true prophet (Deuteronomy 18:22). However, it does not invalidate a true prophet when he or she makes a conditional prediction in the Lord's name (for example, Jonah 3:4–10).

Fourth, people who trust God will turn only to Him for knowledge of the future; they will not resort to alternative occult sources. Biblical law strictly prohibits occult practices (Exodus 22:18 [Hebrew verse 17]; Leviticus 19:26, 31; 20:6, 27; Deuteronomy 18:9–14), as they violate the first of the Ten Commandments: "You shall have no other gods before me" (Exodus 20:3).

"Anointed One," or Messiah

Isaiah 45:1 calls Cyrus the Lord's "anointed," which in Hebrew is *mashiakh*; this word is transliterated into Greek as *messias* and then in English as "messiah." Elsewhere in the Old Testament, the term *mashiakh* is applied to the patriarchs, including Abraham and his descendants (1 Chronicles 16:22; Psalm 105:15), Israelite (high) priests (Leviticus 4:3, 5, 16; 6:22 [Hebrew verse 15]), and Israelite kings (1 Samuel 16:6; 24:6, 10 [Hebrew verses 7, 11]; 2 Samuel 22:51; Psalm 18:50 [Hebrew verse 51]). The Lord also told Elijah to anoint Elisha as the prophet in his place (1 Kings 19:16), although Elisha is not called a *mashiakh*, "anointed one."

These individuals were the highest religious and civil leaders of God's people, whom He chose. For priests and kings, this choice could be signified by a literal, physical act of anointing, performed by a representative of the Lord, such as a prophet. Anointing a person—that is, putting some oil on him—symbolically conferred a divinely designated status upon that individual (for example, Exodus 28:41; 1 Samuel 10:1; 16:13). The main point of anointing was to dedicate the person to God as one who was holy to Him and was to serve a holy function, as affirmed by comparison with the anointing of nonhuman objects to give them a holy status (for example, Genesis 31:13; Exodus 40:9–15; Leviticus 8:10–12).

Only in Isaiah 45:1 is a person outside the line of Abraham—namely, Cyrus—called the Lord's "anointed" (*mashiakh*), although God commissioned Elijah to anoint Hazael as king over Syria (1 Kings 19:15). How could Cyrus, a Persian king, receive this high designation? He was not literally anointed by a Hebrew prophet, but the Lord treated him as a special leader of His people to carry out a holy function. Indeed, Cyrus became king over the Jews when he conquered Babylon, and he accomplished God's holy purpose of freeing the Jewish people from captivity so that they could return to Jerusalem and rebuild the Lord's holy temple (2 Chronicles 36:22, 23). He was not an Israelite deliverer, as kings such as Saul and David were, but he was a deliverer of Israel nonetheless.

The book of Daniel predicts the coming of another *mashiakh* (Daniel 9:25–27), who can be identified as Christ, the ultimate "Anointed One," or Messiah. We have already found prophecies pointing to Christ in Isaiah 7:14; 9:6, 7 (Hebrew verses 5, 6); and 11:1–10. These predictions indicate that He is divine; He would be born of a virgin; He would become a mighty, wise, and eternal ruler from the line of David, establishing peace, justice, and righteousness; the Spirit of the Lord would rest upon Him; and the nations would be drawn to Him. Isaiah 40:3–11 also promises the coming of the powerful but kind Divine King.

Isaiah 42:1–9 further develops the profile of the Messiah, although this passage does not call Him the *mashiakh*. Here He is God's "servant," on whom the Lord puts His Spirit, and "he will bring forth justice to the nations" (verse 1). These aspects identify the Servant with the earlier Messianic prophecies in the book. Additionally, He will be quiet and gentle (verses 2, 3).

"He will not grow faint or be discouraged" (verse 4; literally, "grow dim or be crushed" [NET]). And the Lord says to Him:

> "I will take you by the hand and keep you;
> I will give you as a covenant for the people,
>   a light for the nations,
>   to open the eyes that are blind,
> to bring out the prisoners from the dungeon,
>   from the prison those who sit in darkness" (verses 6, 7).

These words indicate that the Servant would need the Lord's protection ("and keep you"), He would serve as the Mediator of a divine-human covenant, and He would free captives from the darkness of their imprisonment.

Isaiah 42:1–9 is the first of four poems, or songs, commonly called Servant Songs, about the Messiah in the latter half of the book of Isaiah. The other three are found in Isaiah 49:1–13; 50:4–9; and 52:13–53:12. (They will be discussed in the next chapter of the present book.) Isaiah 61:1–3 is also about the Messiah, who is "anointed" by God (verse 1).

Each of the Servant Songs concerns the Individual who is called the Lord's "Servant" (Isaiah 42:1; 49:3; 50:10; 52:13). However, elsewhere in Isaiah 40–66, the nation of God's people is also called the Lord's "servant" (Isaiah 41:8, 9; 42:19; 43:10; 44:1, 2, 21; etc.). What is the relationship between these two servants? John N. Oswalt points out that according to the New Testament, at least some of the Servant Songs "refer to Jesus Christ, the Messiah (Matt. 8:17; 12:18-21; Luke 22:37; 23:33-34; John 12:38; Rev. 7:16-17; etc.)." He explains that in the Servant Songs, "Isaiah is speaking of an individual, almost certainly the Messiah, who will be the ideal Israel. Through his obedient service to God, Israel will be enabled to perform the service of blessing the nations that had been prophesied in Gen. 12:3 and elsewhere."[2]

Already by Isaiah 42, we get the idea that the Messiah would not simply take over by crushing force and cruise to domination without any difficulty. He would be vulnerable, His success would require effort, and He would be kind like Cyrus in that He would bring hope by releasing people from bondage (Isaiah 61:1, compare Luke 4:18). Anyone who reads about the ministry of Jesus in the New Testament can see that Isaiah's profile of Him was accurate—more than seven hundred years earlier!

So what is your future? God knows, but the choice is yours.

---

1. See Roy Gane, *Who's Afraid of the Judgment? The Good News About Christ's Work in the Heavenly Sanctuary* (Nampa, ID: Pacific Press®, 2006), 75, 76.

2. John N. Oswalt, *The Book of Isaiah: Chapters 40-66*, New International Commentary on the Old Testament (Grand Rapids, MI: Eerdmans, 1998), 108.

Ten

Do You Believe What God's Servant Has Done for You?
Isaiah 49, 50, 52, 53

Why does a woman suffering the pain of childbirth want to hold her husband's hand? Why do individuals on their deathbeds wish to be surrounded by their family members? For support. They want to know that someone who cares is with them and that they are not going through the hard experience all alone.

God knows and meets this powerful emotional need when He promises:

"Fear not, for I have redeemed you;
   I have called you by name, you are mine.
When you pass through the waters, I will be with you;
   and through the rivers, they shall not overwhelm you"
     (Isaiah 43:1, 2).

David's Shepherd Psalm contains the same idea: "Even though I walk through the valley of the shadow of death, I will fear no evil, for you are with me" (Psalm 23:4).

A husband who holds his wife's hand during childbirth does not feel labor pains himself. But suffering with someone, or suffering in a similar way at another time, adds another dimension to going through the experience with that person. This forges a strong bond, such as can be seen between combat veterans who have fought and bled together and have risked their lives for each other (for example, 2 Samuel 1:26).

Going through it with us

The second Servant Song in Isaiah 49:1–13 shows that God's Messianic Servant goes through difficulties like those that we experience. This poem has several connections with earlier prophecies—especially the first Servant Song in Isaiah 42:1–9—that identify this Individual as the Divine Messiah. For example, the Lord promises to make Him "a light for the nations" (Isaiah 49:6; compare Isaiah 42:6) and give Him "as a covenant to the people" (Isaiah 49:8; compare Isaiah 42:6), and the Servant will release prisoners to freedom (Isaiah 49:9; compare Isaiah 42:7).

Isaiah 42:4, 6 hint that the Servant may need to overcome some challenges with the Lord's help, but Isaiah 49:4 makes this explicit, quoting the Servant as lamenting,

"I have labored in vain;
    I have spent my strength for nothing and vanity;
yet surely my right is with the LORD,
    and my recompense with my God."

The Divine Servant of the Lord knows, as we do, what it is like to be frustrated and work hard with no apparent result (compare Daniel 9:26: the Messiah "shall have nothing").

Isaiah 49:7 further darkens the Servant's outlook:

Thus says the LORD,
    the Redeemer of Israel and his Holy One,
to one deeply despised, abhorred by the nation,
    the servant of rulers.

But the following words predict a reversal:

> "Kings shall see and arise;
>> princes, and they shall prostrate themselves;
> because of the LORD, who is faithful,
>> the Holy One of Israel, who has chosen you" (verse 7).

The second Servant Song contains an apparent contradiction: in Isaiah 49:3, the Lord calls the Servant "Israel," but in verses 5 and 6, the Servant's task is to restore "Jacob" or "Israel"—that is, the nation of Israel, which descended from Jacob, whose name was changed to Israel (Genesis 32:28)—to God. The Servant can represent the entire nation as the ideal Israel. Compare the way Samson represented all of Israel as a one-man army because the rest of his people were afraid to fight the Philistines (Judges 15:9–15). And God miraculously provided this one man with water in a wilderness (verses 18, 19) as He had done earlier for the entire nation (Exodus 17:5, 6; Numbers 20:7, 8, 11).

As the ideal Israel, the Servant serves as a covenant for and to (literally "of") the people (Isaiah 42:6; 49:8); in other words, He is the Mediator of the divine-human covenant. Even if the other members of the nation fail to keep the covenant, He can represent them before the Lord as the human party to the covenant to maintain it and give them the opportunity to come back to God.

Going through it voluntarily

Like the earlier Servant Songs, the third Song in Isaiah 50:4–9 (referring to the Lord's "servant" in verse 10) affirms the Servant's dependence on God. But there is an additional factor: the Servant listens to God, learns from Him, and obeys Him (verses 4, 5), even if this results in suffering (verse 6; compare Psalm 40:6–8 [Hebrew verses 7–9]).

The previous Servant Song predicts that the Servant will be "deeply despised, abhorred by the nation" (Isaiah 49:7), and the third Song foresees the physical manifestation of this rejection:

> I gave my back to those who strike,
>> and my cheeks to those who pull out the beard;
> I hid not my face
>> from disgrace and spitting (Isaiah 50:6).

Not only would the Servant go through a miserable human experience but He would do so voluntarily. This prophecy was fulfilled when Jesus allowed His tormenters to publicly and physically humiliate Him (Matthew 26:67, 68; 27:28–31; John 19:1). They could not have done anything to Him if He and His Father had not allowed it (Matthew 26:53; John 19:11).

Jesus endured it all, even crucifixion, "despising the shame" (Hebrews 12:2)—that is, despising the despising. Those who treated Him despicably were the shameful ones who needed forgiveness from God (Luke 23:34). Isaiah 50:7 predicts His attitude: "But the Lord GOD helps me; therefore I have not been disgraced." Jesus' enemies were only increasing His honor in the sight of God, whose perspective is what matters.

Those who are treated badly for the sake of Christ can be encouraged by knowing that He has already voluntarily endured suffering for them. When they willingly "bear the reproach he endured" (Hebrews 13:13), they, too, will be honored by God. They can also be assured that He goes through their experience with them (for example, Daniel 3:23–25).

Going through it for us

The fourth Servant Song in Isaiah 52:13–53:12, otherwise known as the Suffering Servant poem, brings Isaiah's predictions of the Messiah to a climax. This amazing prophecy, along with Psalm 22 and Daniel 9:24–27, is one of the clearest and most powerful pictures of the Messiah in the Old Testament, revealing the nature and purpose of His mission in profound depth. Although this poem is generally referred to as the prophecy of Isaiah 53, it actually begins in Isaiah 52:13, where the Lord begins speaking of "my servant."

The poem traces the Suffering Servant's career, beginning by stating the outcome of His success and exaltation (verse 13) and then describing the background behind this conclusion. This gives the poem a shape like that of a trip into and out of the Grand Canyon, starting high and then progressively descending into the depths before going up the other side (compare Philippians 2:5–11).

In addition to highlighting the suffering of the Messiah, the fourth Servant Song reiterates several elements of earlier Messianic prophecies in Isaiah, including the first three Servant Songs, and intensifies some of them. For example, in the first and second Servant Songs, the Lord designates His Servant "as a covenant" for or to "the people" and "a light for the nations" (Isaiah 42:6; 49:6, 8). In the fourth Song, He will "sprinkle many nations" (Isaiah 52:15), apparently referring to the priestly sprinkling of blood and/or water for purification (compare Leviticus 14:7; Numbers 8:7; 19:18, 19), and He "makes intercession for the transgressors" (Isaiah 53:12), serving as a covenant mediator between God and "many" (verses 11, 12) faulty humans.

The major new element that the fourth Servant Song adds is the substitutionary purpose of the Servant's suffering, which culminates in His death. Not only does He voluntarily go through suffering with us in the sense that He endures a hard experience like that which can come upon other human beings, but He also uniquely suffers for us, in place of us, to save many people from the deadly consequence of their sins. He is innocent (Isaiah 53:9; see also Isaiah 50:9), but He is smitten by God Himself as He bears the curse of sin for those who really deserve it (Galatians 3:13).

This gospel message is so amazing that Isaiah 53 repeats it in various ways to drive the message home (verses 4–6, 8, 10–12).

Now we can understand what is behind God's previous offers of mercy, such as in Isaiah 1:18: "Though your sins are like scarlet, they shall be as white as snow." All of these offers are based on the substitutionary sacrifice of God's Divine Servant. The Lord's grace is not cheap; it comes at the infinite cost of His Son.

He shall see His offspring

In Isaiah 53:10, what is the significance of the phrase "he shall see his offspring" (literally "his seed"), which refers to the future generations or descendants of the Servant after His resurrection from death? The fourth Servant Song prophecy was fulfilled in the Divine Christ, as affirmed in Acts 8:28–35, but nowhere in the Bible is there any indication that Jesus Christ had any children in the physical human manner. Christ's offspring, however, can be spiritual, just as those who belong to Christ are the spiritual offspring of Abraham (Galatians 3:29). Remember also that Christ is the Creator (John 1:3; Hebrews 1:2) and that Adam was "the son of God" (Luke 3:38) because God Himself—that is, Christ—created him. So as the Creator, Christ the Messiah is the "Everlasting Father" (Isaiah 9:6 [Hebrew verse 5]) of the entire human race, which is why His death for all of us is justly equivalent to all of us dying (compare Hebrews 7:9, 10, where Abraham's action of paying tithe to Melchizedek can be viewed as representing that of Levi, his descendant).

Christ is not only our Creator; because of His sacrifice, He is also our Re-creator, who gives us eternal life if we accept the transforming new birth through the Holy Spirit that He has made possible (John 3:3–8; Romans 6:4; 8:1–17; Titus 3:4–7). Therefore, we are "children of God" (Romans 8:16, 17; 1 John 3:1, 10) and Christ's descendants in this sense, to which Isaiah 53:10 refers.

There is more to the meaning of the phrase "he shall see his offspring" in Isaiah 53:10. In Daniel 9:26, the Messiah is "cut off." Here the Hebrew verb is from the root *k-r-t* (unlike in Isaiah

53:8, where "cut off" is from the verb *g-z-r*, referring to the Servant's death); elsewhere, *k-r-t* often refers to a terminal penalty for a serious sin, which is carried out by God Himself (for example, Genesis 17:14; Exodus 31:14; Leviticus 17:10; 18:29; Numbers 15:30). The penalty is not simply banishment or death but goes beyond death. This is shown by the sequence in Leviticus 20:2, where a person who "gives any of his children to Molech" shall be put to death by stoning, and in verse 3, God will set His face against the same person ("that man") and "will cut him off [verb *k-r-t*] from among his people." An Israelite could be punished after his death by losing his descendants, through whom his life would have continued in a sense (for example, 2 Samuel 21:1–14). Thus, to be "cut off" from among one's people was to lose an ongoing heritage in one's kinship group. This loss of an "afterlife" was like a death after death—a second death.[1]

How could the Messiah be "cut off" (Daniel 9:26)? By losing His afterlife through a second death. In this case, the second death would be equivalent to the final, permanent eradication of sinners identified in the book of Revelation (Revelation 2:11; 20:6, 14; 21:8). This is the death of which Romans 6:23 speaks: "For the wages of sin is death, but the free gift of God is eternal life in Christ Jesus our Lord." On the cross, Christ died the first death of a human being, but to free us from the second death, He must have suffered that as well to take the full penalty for sin in our place. Just dying the first death, which is like sleep (Luke 8:52; John 11:11), could not save us from the second death, which results in eternal nonexistence.

When Christ cried out in anguish on the cross, "My God, my God, why have you forsaken me?" (Matthew 27:46; quoting Psalm 22:1 [Hebrew verse 2]), He was going through a second death excruciating experience of separation from the other Members of the Godhead. This was because God crushed Him (Isaiah 53:10) by making "him to be sin who knew no sin" (2 Corinthians 5:21). Nevertheless, because Christ was actually innocent and bore the sins of others, He uniquely came forth from the experience of the second death, from which there is otherwise no return. Even though He was "cut off," "he shall see his offspring" (Isaiah 53:8, 10).

The righteous and righteousness

The English Standard Version renders Isaiah 53:11 with these words: "By his knowledge shall the righteous one, my servant, make many to be accounted righteous." However, the New English Translation Bible interprets "by his knowledge" as belonging to the preceding clause: He will be satisfied by His knowledge—that is, "when he understands what he has done." The following words in the original Hebrew literally read: "He will declare righteous a righteous one my servant for the many." The subject of this clause is "my servant," so "my servant will declare righteous a righteous one for the many." But most English versions interpret "a righteous one" as describing in apposition the Lord's servant, as the English Standard Version does: "The righteous one, my servant."

Nevertheless, earlier in the Hebrew Bible, the legal expression "declare righteous a righteous one" is a unit. In Deuteronomy 25:1 and 1 Kings 8:32, a just judge (God in 1 Kings 8) is to declare righteous the righteous or declare wicked the wicked— in other words, acquit, justify, or condemn them according to what they have done. To do otherwise is unjust (Proverbs 17:15; Isaiah 5:23). The judge does not make people innocent or guilty; he recognizes and acknowledges what they already are.

Returning to Isaiah 53:11, God's Servant declares righteous the righteous for many people; that is, He justifies them as innocent, as though they have not committed wrongs. How can He do that when "all we like sheep have gone astray" (verse 6)? The next words in verse 11 have the answer: the Servant "shall bear their iniquities"—that is, the culpabilities or blame resulting from their sins (as in Leviticus 5:1). On this basis alone, before God's law they are now innocent, free from condemnation (Romans 8:1; compare Leviticus 5:6, 10).

This is not divine legal fiction or injustice but reality because of Christ's substitution, not because of what we have done but because of what He has done. God, as the just Judge, has stated literally: "I will not declare righteous the wicked" (Exodus 23:7, author's translation). Christ's sacrifice makes it possible for God to "be just and the justifier of the one who has faith in Jesus" (Romans 3:26). God justifies those who accept the gift of Christ's sacrifice for them by faith, and therefore, they are just or righteous in the sense that they are forgiven. This forgiveness changes their lives, as Jesus said to the woman caught in adultery, "Neither do I condemn you; go, and from now on sin no more" (John 8:11).

What has God's Servant done for you? Have you accepted the Messiah as your righteousness?

---

1. For more on this penalty, see Donald J. Wold, "The Meaning of the Biblical Penalty *Kareth*" (PhD diss., University of California, Berkeley, 1978), 251–255; Jacob Milgrom, *Leviticus 1–16: A New Translation With Introduction and Commentary*, Anchor Bible 3 (New York: Doubleday, 1991), 457–460. See also Psalm 109:13: "May his posterity be cut off; may their names be blotted out in the next generation" (NJPS).

Eleven

Why Not Accept God's Free Gift?
Isaiah 55, 56, 58

Isaiah 55:1 proclaims an invitation:

"Come, everyone who thirsts,
   come to the waters;
and he who has no money,
   come, buy and eat!
Come, buy wine and milk."

This sounds like a contradiction: "He who has no money, come, buy"! How would that sound to a penniless, homeless person? It could seem like cruel mockery. But Isaiah's next words change the picture: "Without money and without price."

Why does Isaiah say "buy" (Hebrew verb from the root *sh-b-r*) when the life-giving liquids are free? The usual meaning of "buy" (including *sh-b-r*) is to obtain something in exchange for payment (compare Genesis 47:14; Deuteronomy 2:6). What payment does Isaiah have in mind? Is this a trick, like many scams that are too good to be true?

The transaction of free salvation

Isaiah means "buy," but the price is zero shekels. The only require-ment is to "come" and accept the free gift, but that is not payment. Why speak of a free gift in this strange way? To emphasize the value of the gift and that accepting it is a transaction—that is, a transfer of something of value that one must accept by choice.

Isaiah's invitation was not for his people to come to him, but to the Lord, who continues His call:

> "Incline your ear, and come to me;
>   hear, that your soul may live;
> and I will make with you an everlasting covenant,
>   my steadfast, sure love for David.
> Behold, I made him a witness to the peoples,
>   a leader and commander for the peoples" (Isaiah 55:3, 4).

Indeed, there are strings attached, but they are good ones. God's interest is not merely to bestow a one-time gift but to restore an ongoing relationship of mutual commitment—"an everlasting covenant" (see also Isaiah 61:8)—in which He would take care of the people forever. He does not want a date; He proposes marriage. The free gift is vastly larger than mere water, wine, and milk (Isaiah 55:1).

If you want to see what kind of relationship the Lord has in mind, remember what He did for David: He exalted David from herding sheep to shepherding His people, Israel (see Psalm 78:70–72), and ruling an empire as a "commander of nations" (Isaiah 55:4, NET). Why? Because God loved him. Now the Lord, simi-larly motivated by love, offers the same kind of covenant to the Judahites in the time of Isaiah. He wants to glorify them to a position of leadership over other nations, who would come to them when they call (verse 5) as sheep come to a shepherd when he or she calls. God does not expect the people of Judah to accept His offer by blind faith, but in view of His track record with David.

Accepting a gift from the giver requires effort. This effort involves cooperating with God to receive His gift of forgiveness and salvation. It requires leaving some things behind: "Let the wicked forsake his way, and the unrighteous man his thoughts" (verse 7).

It is difficult to understand God's compassion because we have rebelled against Him. Would we do the same if we were in His place? Nevertheless, He assures us that His mercy toward us goes far beyond our own thinking:

"For my thoughts are not your thoughts,
neither are your ways my ways, declares the LORD.
For as the heavens are higher than the earth,
so are my ways higher than your ways
and my thoughts than your thoughts" (verses 8, 9).

We cannot and do not need to understand the full mystery of why and how God saves us. We just need to accept the gift.

It would not make sense to refuse the gift or try to work and pay for an insufficient and faulty alternative (compare verse 2). No person, no matter how rich, can "give to God the price of his life" (Psalm 49:7 [Hebrew verse 8]). God has paid the terrible, blood-drenched cost of giving us mercy with full justice through the second-death experience of His Suffering Servant (Isaiah 53; Daniel 9:26). If we accept His gift, any toil, tears, or sweat that we put forth is *only part of receiving the gift*. It is never reimbursing God for even a fraction of what He has given, which is free for us, "without money and without price" (Isaiah 55:1).

Salvation available for everyone
Isaiah 56 begins,

Thus says the LORD:
"Keep justice, and do righteousness,

for soon my salvation will come,
    and my righteousness be revealed" (verse 1).

The combination of the Hebrew terms for "justice" (*mishpat*) and "righteousness" (*tsedaqah*) is frequent in the Old Testament, including in Isaiah. The two words carry a blended idea, usually the concept of human beings treating others with fairness (2 Samuel 8:15). Near the beginning of the book of Isaiah, the words "Zion shall be redeemed by justice [*mishpat*], and those in her who repent, by righteousness [*tsedaqah*]" (Isaiah 1:27) refer to social justice in opposition to social injustices, such as violence, corruption, and oppression (verses 21–26; see also Isaiah 5:7 in the context of the rest of chapter 5).

God sets a good example for humans: "But the LORD of hosts is exalted in justice, and the Holy God shows himself holy in righteousness" (Isaiah 5:16). He "is not partial and takes no bribe. He executes justice for the fatherless and the widow, and loves the sojourner, giving him food and clothing" (Deuteronomy 10:17, 18).

The Lord pronounces a blessing on the person who "does this" (Isaiah 56:2)—that is, treats others fairly and keeps the Sabbath holy (verses 1, 2). The following verses make the blessing available to anyone who is faithful to the Lord, even if they are not Israelites (verses 3–8). God chose Abraham and his descendants not to limit salvation to them but to privilege them with the responsibility of serving as a channel of revelation through which people of all nations would be blessed (Genesis 12:3; 22:18).

From the beginning, the nation of Israel had non-Israelites dwelling among it, with whom it could share the Lord's blessings. A "mixed multitude" left Egypt with the Israelites (Exodus 12:38), and the divine laws for Israel that are recorded in the Pentateuch (five books of Moses) repeatedly refer to immigrants (Hebrew *ger*) living with them. These people were not required or forced to convert to the worship of Israel's God, YHWH, but they were not to show disrespect to Him by violating His laws (Exodus 12:19).

God drew foreigners into His community. If they wished, immigrants could celebrate the Passover festival with the Israelites if they (that is, the males) were circumcised (Exodus 12:48). They could also offer sacrifices to the Lord (Leviticus 17:8, 9). God's law protected and benefited immigrants, along with widows and orphans, who tended to be poor and vulnerable to oppression (Exodus 22:21–24 [Hebrew verses 20–23]; 23:9; Leviticus 19:10). This kind of protection is unique in the ancient Near East; none of the other ancient Near Eastern law collections, such as the laws of Hammurabi, the Hittite laws, and the Middle Assyrian laws, include concern for helping foreigners.

Biblical law went even further: "You shall treat the stranger who sojourns with you as the native among you, and you shall love him as yourself, for you were strangers in the land of Egypt" (Leviticus 19:34). This is remarkable, extending the principle of Leviticus 19:18—"You shall love your neighbor as yourself"—to non-Israelites as Jesus did (Luke 10:29–37) and pointing ahead to Paul's sweeping statement of gospel equality and unity: "There is neither Jew nor Greek, there is neither slave nor free, there is no male and female, for you are all one in Christ Jesus. And if you are Christ's, then you are Abraham's offspring, heirs according to promise" (Galatians 3:28, 29).

Racism, xenophobia, class distinctions, and elitism have no place in the religion of the true God or the lifestyle and attitudes of His people, who are all brothers and sisters created in the image of God. True Christians provide generous kindness and assistance to foreigners, including immigrants, and draw others into fellowship with them, as Jesus ate with all kinds of people (Matthew 9:10–13).

Isaiah 56:3–8 builds on the Pentateuchal background in a magnificent manifesto of inclusiveness addressed to foreigners and also to eunuchs. In this passage, the Hebrew word for "foreigner" refers to foreigners in general, not just resident aliens. If any foreigners joined themselves to the Lord, He would accept them without reservation, gathering them along with the Israelites who have been dispersed, apparently by exile (verse 8), and giving them joy in His "house of prayer" (verse 7). The temple had always been a place of prayer (for example, 1 Samuel 1:9–16; 1 Kings 8:22–54). The Lord makes explicit and emphasizes that His house of prayer is "for all peoples" (Isaiah 56:7). God's hospitality is universal: Everyone who desires a relationship with Him is welcome at His house. This is a model for Christian church congregations: Everyone who wants to worship the Lord should be welcome.

In Isaiah 56:3–8, God encourages eunuchs, along with foreigners. According to biblical law, "No one whose testicles are crushed or whose male organ is cut off shall enter the assembly [Hebrew *qahal*] of the LORD" (Deuteronomy 23:1 [Hebrew verse 2])—that is, the community of full-status male Israelites who governed the nation. Israelites were expected to have children to continue the legacies of their families, including ownership of property in the Promised Land, from their ancestors to their descendants (for example, Numbers 27:1–11; Deuteronomy 25:5–10; Ruth 4). It is unlikely that an Israelite male would choose to become a eunuch, although this could happen as a result of a severe accident.

However, when the kings of Israel and Judah had harems, at least some of them used eunuchs as their palace servants (2 Kings 9:32; Jeremiah 29:2; 34:19; 38:7), in accordance with ancient Near Eastern practice. This was to prevent any of these men, who could be high officials near ladies of the royal court (for example, Esther 2:3, 14, 15), from having sex with any of these women, including in an attempt to seize the throne (compare 2 Samuel 16:21, 22; 1 Kings 2:13–25). A eunuch could never become a king because he could not have an heir.

Isaiah reported to Hezekiah that when the Babylonians

would take Judah, "Some of your own sons . . . shall be eunuchs in the palace of the king of Babylon" (Isaiah 39:7; paralleling 2 Kings 20:18). Not only would such males be cut off from their people in the sense that they would be captives in a foreign land, but they would also be permanently cut off from being full members of the community of God's people because they were denied a legacy, or "afterlife," through having children.

Nevertheless, God gave hope to eunuchs by telling them that if they were faithful to Him and kept His covenant, He would give them an even greater legacy than children: "An everlasting name that shall not be cut off [Hebrew k-r-t]" (Isaiah 56:5). They would be part of the Lord's covenant community in a higher sense. Indeed, Scripture has immortalized the faithfulness of some eunuchs, such as Ebed-melech, the Ethiopian eunuch who rescued the prophet Jeremiah from a cistern with mud at the bottom (Jeremiah 38:6–13), and another Ethiopian eunuch, "a court official of Candace, queen of the Ethiopians, who was in charge of all her treasure" (Acts 8:27), who accepted the gospel of Jesus Christ in Isaiah 53 as Philip explained it to him (Acts 8:28–39).

The custom of making males into eunuchs has ceased, but the principle of Isaiah's message is relevant to members of God's community of faith who do not have children. Their legacy does not depend on having a family but on being loyal to God, as Jeremiah was faithful during his long ministry as a single person because the Lord commanded him: "You shall not take a wife, nor shall you have sons or daughters in this place" (Jeremiah 16:2).

Benefits of true fasting and Sabbath keeping

The Lord promises that those who "keep justice," keep the Sabbath, and keep their hands "from doing any evil" will be blessed (Isaiah 56:1, 2). Isaiah 58 develops this theme by combining it with a stern rebuke against the Judahites for their religious hypocrisy, as in Isaiah 1:10–17. Whereas Isaiah 56:2

refers to the weekly Sabbath (see also verse 4), Isaiah 58 addresses observance of the Day of Atonement sabbath, the only ceremonial sabbath on which all work was prohibited as on the weekly Sabbath, and the people were to practice self-denial that included fasting (Leviticus 16:29, 31; 23:26–32; compare Psalm 35:13).

The Day of Atonement was the holiest day of the Israelite liturgical year because it was the only day on which the high priest was permitted to enter the Most Holy Place of the temple (called the "Holy Place" in Leviticus 16). He would ritually purge the entire sanctuary from the sins and physical ritual impurities of the Israelites by applications of sacrificial blood (verses 14–16, 18, 19). As a result, the Israelites who demonstrated their loyalty to God by keeping this sabbath and humbling themselves through self-denial received final moral purification from their sins (verses 29–31)—that is, the sins for which the Lord had already forgiven them through sacrifices (Leviticus 4:20, 26, 31, etc.) prefiguring Christ's sacrifice (John 1:29). The people did not need to be forgiven all over again; instead, the rituals of this day demonstrated that God's justice in mercifully forgiving them was vindicated. He was just when He justified the right people—those who had faith (Romans 3:26).[1]

The Day of Atonement on the tenth day of the seventh month was Israel's annual Judgment Day; it separated the loyal from anyone who disloyally failed to abstain from work and practice self-denial. Such a person would be "cut off" and/or destroyed by God (Leviticus 23:29, 30).

It is against this solemn background that we can feel the full force of the rebuke in Isaiah 58. The chapter begins with these words:

"Cry aloud; do not hold back;
    lift up your voice like a trumpet;
declare to my people their transgression,
    to the house of Jacob their sins" (verse 1).

This statement is ironic for two reasons. First, on the first day of the seventh month, ten days before the Day of Atonement, there was "a memorial proclaimed with blast of trumpets" (Leviticus 23:24; "trumpets" is implied in the Hebrew). This ushered in the festival season of the seventh month and prepared for the Day of Atonement. Now God commands the prophet to rebuke his people with a "voice like a trumpet." Second, the Hebrew terms used here for moral faults— "transgression," that is, rebellious sin (*pesha'*), and "sin" (*khatta't*)—are the same and in the same order as in Leviticus 16:16, where the high priest is to remove these evils from the Most Holy Place. On the Day of Atonement, when the high priest was removing the sins of the people from the sanctuary, the people were still committing the same kinds of sins!

The Judahites were acting righteous by following God's instruction to practice self-denial on the Day of Atonement (Isaiah 58:3a; see also verse 2), but at the same time, they were seeking their own pleasure, thereby breaking the sabbath (compare verse 13), oppressing their workers, and getting into arguments and even fistfights (verses 3b, 4a). This is exactly the opposite of keeping justice, keeping the sabbath, and keeping hands (including fists!) "from doing any evil" (Isaiah 56:1, 2). If this is what the Judahites regarded as a fast day because they went through the motions of fake humility, God wanted nothing to do with it (Isaiah 58:4b, 5).

God was not repealing His commands to practice self-denial and abstain from work on the Day of Atonement. Rather, in the remainder of Isaiah 58, He explains the meaning behind the genuine fasting (verses 6–12) and sabbath rest (verses 13, 14) that He accepts. Both of these practices reflect humility before God as the Creator and Provider of food (Genesis 1, 2) and humility in relation to other human beings because fasting and rest make everyone equal. Nobody eats more or better or does more important work than anyone else because nobody eats or works.

Humility is crucial for our relationship with God, who dwells "with him who is of a contrite and lowly spirit" (Isaiah 57:15).

Acknowledging dependence on God and commonality with other people, as shown by fasting, implies that as God provides for His people's needs, they should help others to meet the kinds of needs that they have in common with them. Thus, God's people should not only treat others fairly but also set free those who are oppressed (including from oppressors who may not appreciate this, such as slave owners and human traffickers!), feed the hungry, house the homeless, and clothe the naked (Isaiah 58:6, 7; see also verses 9b, 10a; Matthew 25:31–46; James 1:27).

God is generous to those who are generous to others, promising them wonderful blessings: restoration, answers to prayers, guidance, and satisfaction (Isaiah 58:8, 9a, 10b–12).

Isaiah 58:13, 14 concludes the chapter by addressing the topic of the sabbath. The primary context is the Day of Atonement, but the principles in these verses also apply to the weekly Sabbath. The verses express conditions and results: "If" you obey God's instructions (verse 13), "then" you will enjoy the subsequent blessings (verse 14). The conditions are as follows:

> "If you turn back your foot from the Sabbath,
>   from doing your pleasure on my holy day,
> and call the Sabbath a delight
>   and the holy day of the LORD honorable;
> if you honor it, not going your own ways,
>   or seeking your own pleasure, or talking idly" (verse 13).

Turning "back your foot from the Sabbath" means not trampling on it to profane it by breaking the command to keep it holy by resting on it (for example, Exodus 20:8–11). The Hebrew word for "your [own] pleasure" (Isaiah 58:13) is the same as in verse 3, where the hypocritical Judahites were seeking their own pleasure—that is, what they wanted to do on the Day of

Atonement sabbath, thereby breaking the sabbath. Since the sabbath command was not to do any work (Leviticus 16:29), it is clear that they were doing something that would be considered work, along with oppressing their workers, which could involve forcing them to work on this rest day.

The correct interpretation of the original Hebrew text about not doing your own "pleasure" (Isaiah 58:13), which goes against centuries of Christian (but not Jewish) misunderstanding and assumptions based on English translations, does not rule out enjoying yourself on the weekly Sabbath, so long as it is in harmony with God's command to rest, including not engaging in work-related talk, which is idle or "idol" talk on the Sabbath. Isaiah 58:13 does not forbid the pleasure of sex within marriage during Sabbath hours at all, just as it does not prohibit the enjoyment of good food, Bible study, fellowship, music in honor of God, preaching, or nature walks.

There is a close relationship between keeping the Sabbath and our relationship with God: those who "call the Sabbath a delight" (verse 13) will "take delight in the LORD" (verse 14). His day is our time for special, exquisite pleasure with Him. He blessed the seventh-day Sabbath and "made it holy" in the beginning (Genesis 2:3), and its blessing goes to all who participate in its holiness by dedicating these sacred hours to Him. Like God's salvation, the Sabbath is free, and it is for everyone. Why not accept God's extravagant free gift?

---

1. For an explanation of the Day of Atonement service and its meaning, see Roy Gane, *The Sanctuary and Salvation: The Practical Significance of Christ's Sacrifice and Priesthood* (Madrid, Spain: Editorial Safeliz, 2019), 193–209, 217–222, 231–237; Roy Gane, *Leviticus, Numbers*, NIV Application Commentary (Grand Rapids, MI: Zondervan, 2004), 270–297.

Twelve

How Soon Can We Get Together?
Isaiah 59-61

Have you ever had something get in the way of your relationship with another person? God has that problem too.

> Behold, the LORD's hand is not shortened, that it cannot save,
>   or his ear dull, that it cannot hear;
> but your iniquities have made a separation
>   between you and your God,
> and your sins have hidden his face from you
>   so that he does not hear (Isaiah 59:1, 2).

Those who cherish their sins should not expect the Lord to respond to their prayers (Psalm 66:18).

Separation caused by sin has a remedy

God can help us only if we give up the sins that separate us from Him (compare Judges 10:9–16). We may not have the strength to give them up by ourselves, but we need to be willing to give them up and cooperate with Him as He removes them for us or helps us to remove them because we cannot take them to His eternal kingdom of everlasting life and perfect harmony.

The Lord saves "people from their sins" (Matthew 1:21)—not in their sins. If He were to bless those who disregard His life-giving principles, He would send a dangerous false message to the world that His principles do not matter. He would also encourage and strengthen harmful behaviors, including oppressive actions, and He would prolong the suffering caused by sin.

Do you want God's New Jerusalem and the new earth (Revelation 21, 22) to be safe neighborhoods? Would they be safe if God saved people who never let go of their selfishness? Would they be safe if you were there?

The notion that God will save everyone who is "nice," miraculously taking away the sins they cherish in order to make them perfect, is a whimsical, unbiblical, and false gospel believed by millions of people. It is not enough to be "nice." God does not violate human free will by taking sins away from people against their will. If they have chosen to fully give themselves to Him and they make a mistake, He will graciously forgive them when they confess (Micah 7:18; 1 John 1:9; 2:1, 2). However, there is no evidence in the Bible that the Lord forces characters on people that they have not chosen.

Our characters are works in progress—sometimes bumpy progress—throughout our lives, but God knows what kind of people we have chosen to become by accepting the transforming power of His Holy Spirit (John 3:5–8; Romans 5:5; 8:4–17; Titus 3:4–7), and He respects our choice. God's judgment before Christ's second coming (Daniel 7:9, 10; Revelation 14:7) does not change our characters; it acknowledges what they are (compare Revelation 22:11). Receiving perfect, immortal bodies at Christ's second coming (1 Corinthians 15:51–55) will not change the characters that we have chosen. Rather, this will facilitate the completion of those characters by taking away moral weakness that now resides in our faulty, mortal bodies (compare James 1:14, 15).

Therefore, the choices we make matter—not only the big choices but all the little ones that confront us each day. Together, they develop our lives' moral texture that forms our characters.

What does God want us to choose? In agreement with Isaiah, Micah (a contemporary of his) summarized:

> He has told you, O man, what is good;
>   and what does the LORD require of you
> but to do justice, and to love kindness,
>   and to walk humbly with your God? (Micah 6:8).

Justice, kindness or mercy, and humility are the three aspects of unselfish love that Jesus demonstrated when He humbled Himself to come and live, minister, teach, and die among us. God wants nothing less than for us to choose in this life, and demonstrate our commitment to that choice by the way we live, to live forever and by free choice in harmony with His character of unselfish love. Nothing less than that will prevent sin from arising again a second time (compare Nahum 1:9).

Restoration of God's glorious presence

Sins separating people from God cause darkness and gloom (Isaiah 59:9), but His redemption brings light: "Arise, shine, for your light has come, and the glory of the LORD has risen upon you" (Isaiah 60:1).

We know that the words of Isaiah 60:1 are addressed to Zion by following the discourse to verse 14, where "you" is referred to as "the City of the LORD, the Zion of the Holy One of Israel." Isaiah 60 is about Jerusalem's restoration to glory, reflecting God's glory. Even though "darkness shall cover the earth," the Lord's "glory will be seen upon" Zion (verse 2), attracting people of other nations to its light (verse 3). This would result in non-Israelites, including people from Sheba, bringing wealth to Jerusalem and praising the Lord (verses 5–9; see also verses 13,

17), as in the glorious days of King Solomon when the queen of Sheba visited him (1 Kings 10). Among this wealth would be many animals that the Lord would accept as sacrifices on His altar at His splendid temple, which He would glorify (Isaiah 60:7). The fact that He would accept them indicates that they would be offered with sincere, wholehearted devotion, not with the earlier hypocrisy that had caused God to reject the worship practiced by His people (Isaiah 1:11–15).

Rather than trying to conquer Jerusalem, foreigners would build its walls, and their kings would serve its needs (Isaiah 60:10). Its gates would always be open to receive wealth and kings from the nations (verse 11); they would not need to be closed for defense due to a threat.

The aspect of God's glory that attracts people of other nations is more than literal light. Other Old Testament passages predict that foreigners would be attracted to the Israelites because of the wisdom of the laws that God had given them (Deuteronomy 4:6–8) and to the Lord's temple in Jerusalem for basically the same reason (Isaiah 2:3; paralleled by Micah 4:2). Isaiah appeals to his own Judahite people to "walk in the light of the LORD" (Isaiah 2:5), living according to God's wise and just teachings. The psalmist notes that the Lord's light is His instruction for successful and peaceful living: "Your word is a lamp to my feet and a light to my path" (Psalm 119:105).

Most modern people, including many Christians, are ignorant concerning the practical value of God's wise instructions in the Bible. While many of His directives come to us in the context of an ancient Near Eastern culture and many of them are obsolete in the sense that we cannot and do not need to literally observe them (for example, the ritual practices connected to the sanctuary), all of them represent or encapsulate ongoing principles that can guide us to success and make us "wise for salvation" and "complete, equipped for every good work" in various areas of life (2 Timothy 3:15, 17).[1] Other people will be attracted to the glory of God's love and wisdom that shines through us. "Arise, shine, for your light has come, and the glory of the LORD has risen upon you" (Isaiah 60:1)! "Let your light shine before others, so that they may see your good works and give glory to your Father who is in heaven" (Matthew 5:16).

The restored prominence and wealth of Jerusalem would not be for its own self-pride or elitism but to reveal God: "You shall know that I, the LORD, am your Savior and your Redeemer, the Mighty One of Jacob" (Isaiah 60:16; compare Isaiah 59:20). God's chosen people had lost sight of Him, but what He alone accomplished for them in spite of themselves (compare Isaiah 59:16–21) demonstrated who He really was.

Let us briefly turn to the story of Manasseh for an example of God's true character. Compare the response of Manasseh, the most abominably wicked king of Judah (2 Chronicles 33), who repented and prayed to the Lord when the cruel Assyrians captured him. When God restored him to Jerusalem and his throne, "then Manasseh knew that the LORD was God" (verse 13).

What does it mean to know that the Lord is God and that He is the Savior and Redeemer? Manasseh must have had at least intellectual knowledge about God because he was the son of Hezekiah, who was faithful to the Lord (2 Chronicles 29–32). But he did not personally know God or believe in His power and character because he was deceived by sin and did not allow God to have any role in his life. It was when he experienced God's deliverance from terrifying circumstances utterly beyond his control (2 Chronicles 33:11) that sin's deception regarding God was ripped from him.

The same thing happened to the people of Judah, who were complicit in Manasseh's guilt, paying no attention to the Lord's messages (2 Chronicles 33:9, 10). They had mental and spiritual density and stubbornness of epic proportions, so it took the Exile, and God's deliverance from it, to wake them up.

Unfortunately, modern people may not be much different. Is it necessary for us to go through nasty experiences? Can we not learn from what happened to others such as Manasseh and the people of Judah? Those who believe the Bible can learn the easy and inexpensive way (the cost of a Bible and some time) that the Lord is God. If we do not learn that way, Divine Providence can work with experiences in our lives to teach us, but the "tuition" can be expensive.

After the Exile, the Jews—a later name for the people of Judah—returned to their homeland, and they rebuilt Jerusalem and the Lord's temple (see especially Ezra and Nehemiah). The second temple became glorious, and people of other nations came to it, including converts to Judaism (for example, John 12:20; Acts 2:5–11). So the prophecies of restoration were fulfilled to a significant extent.

Nevertheless, the prophecy that the Lord's glory in Jerusalem would attract the nations goes beyond what was fulfilled in the second temple period. Unfulfilled elements in Isaiah 60 include foreigners bringing "the wealth of the nations, with their kings led in procession" (verse 11) and the following:

The sun shall be no more
   your light by day,
nor for brightness shall the moon
   give you light;
but the LORD will be your everlasting light,
   and your God will be your glory (verse 19;
      see also verse 20).

If these words had applied to Jerusalem during the time of the second temple, they would have been a hyperbolic and metaphorical way to emphasize that the light of God's continuing glory would eclipse the glory of anything else. However, we find the ultimate fulfillment of Isaiah 60 in the description of the New Jerusalem in Revelation 21: "And the city has no need of sun or moon to shine on it, for the glory of God gives it light, and its lamp is the Lamb. By its light will the nations walk, and the kings of the earth will bring their glory into it, and its gates will never be shut by day—and there will be no night there. They will bring into it the glory and the honor of the nations" (verses 23–26).

Messianic Minister of restoration

Isaiah 61 begins with a beautiful speech:

> The Spirit of the Lord GOD is upon me,
>   because the LORD has anointed me
> to bring good news to the poor;
>   he has sent me to bind up the brokenhearted,
> to proclaim liberty to the captives,
>   and the opening of the prison to those who are bound
>   (verse 1).

The Speaker here "possesses the divine spirit, is God's spokesman, and is sent to release prisoners from bondage. The evidence suggests he is the God's special servant, described earlier in the servant songs (see 42:1-4, 7; 49:2, 9; 50:4; see also 51:16)."[2] Of special note in this regard is Isaiah 42, where the Lord puts His Spirit upon His Servant [verse 1], who releases captives (verse 7), and Isaiah 49, where the Servant also frees prisoners (verse 9).

Isaiah 61 continues, "To proclaim the year of the LORD's favor, and the day of vengeance of our God; to comfort all who mourn" (verse 2). These elements of the Servant's prophetic message relate to the message of restoration in chapter 60. For example, the Lord's favor is His acceptance (Hebrew *ratson*) of something pleasing to Him, as in Isaiah 60:7, where sacrifices "shall come up with acceptance [*ratson*]" on His altar. This connection suggests that the year of His favor is the time when His relationship with His people, signified by the acceptable sacrifices, would be restored. Isaiah 60:12 also predicts a time of God's vengeance: "For the nation and kingdom that will not serve you [Zion] shall perish; those nations shall be utterly laid waste."

God's special Servant in Isaiah 61 is His Minister of restoration, who gives gentle comfort and encouragement (compare Isaiah 42:2, 3). The fact that the Lord has anointed this Servant (Isaiah 61:1) makes Him the "Anointed One," the Messiah, who is divine (compare Isaiah 9:6 [Hebrew verse 5]). He would do even more than Cyrus, God's foreign anointed one (Isaiah 45:1), who would let the exiled Jews go free (verse 13; 2 Chronicles 36:23).

If Cyrus would release the captive Jews to end their Babylonian exile, what prisoners would God's Messianic Servant set free? It appears that His role would address a different situation. Luke 4:16–21 confirms this. In the synagogue at Nazareth, Jesus read from the beginning of Isaiah 61 down to the words "to proclaim the year of the LORD's favor" (Isaiah 61:2). Then He made a stunning pronouncement: "Today this Scripture has been fulfilled in your hearing" (Luke 4:21)! In other words, He announced that He was God's Messianic Servant, although He stopped short of reading "the day of vengeance of our God" (Isaiah 61:2), which was still in the future.

Jesus did "bring good news to the poor" (Isaiah 61:1; compare Matthew 11:5), including the "poor in spirit," letting them know that they were blessed by possessing nothing less than "the kingdom of heaven" (Matthew 5:3). Jesus did "bind up the brokenhearted" and comfort mourners (Isaiah 61:1, 2), most notably when He raised their dead relatives to life (Matthew 9:25; Luke 7:14, 15; John 11:44). He also proclaimed "liberty to the captives" (Isaiah 61:1) who were bound by sin, Satan, and demons. These were stronger than prisons made of stones or bricks and iron bars (Luke 8:29).

How Soon Can We Get Together?

Jesus proclaimed "the year of the LORD's favor" (Isaiah 61:2), not merely in terms of God's acceptance of animal sacrifices but concerning the sacrifice of Himself (Isaiah 53). This is the only sacrifice that can actually restore our relationship with God so that our separation from Him can be healed (Hebrews 10:1–18), and one day He will dwell with us (Revelation 21:3). Then we will be able to walk and talk with Him as Adam and Eve did in the beginning. How soon can we get together?

---

1. For details, see Roy E. Gane, *Old Testament Law for Christians: Original Context and Enduring Application* (Grand Rapids, MI: Baker Academic, 2017).

2. Note 2 for Isaiah 61:1, NET Bible.

Thirteen

Where Do You Want to Be?
Isaiah 64-66

God laments, "I was ready to be sought by those who did not ask for me; I was ready to be found by those who did not seek me" (Isaiah 65:1). He is waiting for His prodigal children to come home (compare Luke 15:11–32).

Readiness to redeem

Christ waits while He knocks on the doors of our hearts (Revelation 3:20). If anyone has the power and right to force His way in, it is He, our Creator (John 1:3; Hebrews 1:2) and Redeemer (Galatians 3:13; 4:4, 5). But unlike sin and Satan, which lurk at the door and look for an opportunity to break or sneak in (compare Genesis 4:7), Jesus stands outside and waits, respecting our free choice. It is Jesus, not sin, who gives us true freedom (John 8:31, 32, 36).

The only freedom that sin ultimately gives is freedom from anything good, including well-being and happiness. God's prodigal Israelite nation discovered that hard reality when Jerusalem was desolated, the temple was burned, and all of their pleasant places became ruins (see Isaiah 64:10, 11).

Isaiah 64:12 begs God, "Will you restrain yourself at these

things, O Lᴏʀᴅ? Will you keep silent, and afflict us so terribly?"
God answers that He has been ready to help all along, but there
is a problem:

> I was ready to be sought . . .
> I spread out my hands all the day
>   to a rebellious people,
> who walk in a way that is not good,
>   following their own devices;
> a people who provoke me
>   to my face continually (Isaiah 65:1–3; see also
>   verses 4–7, 11; Isaiah 66:3, 17).

Spreading out one's hands is a gesture of petition, usually by an
inferior to a superior (for example, Psalm 143:6; Isaiah 1:15),
but here God humbles Himself to plead for His people to come
back to Him.

To help people make intelligent choices regarding their own
destinies, God vividly sets the contrasting options before them:

> "Behold, my servants shall eat,
>   but you shall be hungry;
> behold, my servants shall drink,
>   but you shall be thirsty
> behold, my servants shall rejoice,
>   but you shall be put to shame;
> behold, my servants shall sing for gladness of heart,
>   but you shall cry out for pain of heart
>   and shall wail for breaking of spirit.
> You shall leave your name to my chosen for a curse,
>   and the Lord Gᴏᴅ will put you to death,
>   but his servants he will call by another name"
>   (Isaiah 65:13–15).

As Moses put it, "See, I have set before you today life and good, death and evil" (Deuteronomy 30:15). God is there all along (James 1:17). The choice is up to you.

Does God destroy the wicked?

In our modern world, where many view capital punishment as harsh—even for murder, it is hard for some to accept that God puts to death those who oppose Him. But Isaiah says that He does: "But you who forsake the LORD . . . I will destine you to the sword, and all of you shall bow down to the slaughter" (Isaiah 65:11, 12). Addressing the same group, the Lord says, "The Lord GOD will put you to death" (verse 15; see also Isaiah 66:16: "those slain by the LORD"). It is hard to imagine a more explicit statement than that.

God punishes people and puts them to death in different ways. In Isaiah 10:5, 6, Assyria is the "rod" of God's anger that He sends against the "godless" Israelites. He would allow the Assyrians to defeat, afflict, and kill those who had been His people, rather than continue His protection, because they had rejected Him, and there was nothing more that He could do for them (Isaiah 5:4, 5). They had given up God and His law, so He gave them up to this world's "law of the jungle," which only respects predatory force.

Removing His protection is not the only way God kills those who rebel against Him. When the Assyrians threatened Jerusalem and Hezekiah prayed for deliverance (Isaiah 37), "the angel of the LORD went out and struck down 185,000 in the camp of the Assyrians" (verse 36; see also 2 Kings 19:35; 2 Chronicles 32:21). The angel was God's agent, acting according to His will. Yes, God slays the wicked—sometimes to save other people from their oppression. "God is love" (1 John 4:8, 16), which includes justice as well as mercy (Exodus 34:6-7), a concept that many or even most people do not comprehend. The Lord does not want any to perish, but desires that all should come to repentance (2 Peter 3:9). However, when there is nothing more that He can do (Isaiah 5:4), He carries out His "strange deed" of destruction (Isaiah 28:21). It is "strange" because He does not want to do it, but it is a "deed/act."

God takes responsibility for destroying the wicked, whether He does it directly Himself, as in the Great Flood (Genesis 7); the annihilation of Sodom and Gomorrah (Genesis 19); the slaughter of the Egyptian firstborn (Exodus 12); the obliteration of Korah, Dathan, Abiram, and their associates (Numbers 16); and the final destruction after the millennium (Revelation 20); or whether He uses His agents, such as a destroying angel or messenger (Isaiah 37:36) or the Israelites when He commissioned them to wipe out the nations of Canaan (Deuteronomy 7:1, 2; 20:16, 17; Joshua 6:21; 10:28; etc.).

The book of Isaiah continues the contrast between the redemption of the loyal and the destruction of the disloyal to its end. After portraying a glorious future for those who are saved (Isaiah 66:18–23), the book ends with this dark and macabre picture: "And they [the saved people] shall go out and look on the dead bodies of the men who have rebelled against me. For their worm shall not die, their fire shall not be quenched, and they shall be an abhorrence to all flesh" (verse 24). The words "their worm shall not die" mean "the maggots that eat them will not die" (verse 24, NET).

Is this unquenchable fire the everlasting hell that billions of Christians believe in? Revelation 14:10, 11 speaks of torment "with fire and sulfur" and that "the smoke of their torment goes up forever and ever, and they have no rest, day or night," but the fact that in Isaiah 66:24 the rebels have become "dead bodies" (compare Malachi 4:3: "ashes under the soles of your feet") indicates that their torment lasts only as long as they remain alive, and then they die. The concepts of unquenchable fire and living maggots simply emphasize that these consuming agents do their work of destruction until the task is completely finished.[1]

Complete destruction is also borne out in Jude 7, where "Sodom and Gomorrah and the surrounding cities . . . serve as an example by undergoing a punishment of eternal fire." There is no fire still burning there after thousands of years. The expressions "eternal fire" (Jude 7) and smoke that "goes up forever and ever" (Revelation 14:11) mean that the fire destroys everything.

The unbiblical doctrine of an ever-burning hell is a satanic myth that makes God into an unimaginably sadistic monster. The biblical hell does not exist now; it is the fire that God will ignite on the surface of planet Earth, which will become a "lake of fire" (Revelation 20:14, 15). By this comprehensive destruction after the millennium, He will purge the universe of sin, sinners, Satan, and death (Revelation 20). After the fire has done its work so that all dead bodies will be gone, He will re-create the same earth into our perfect, eternal home (Revelation 21; 22).

A new creation

God predicts through Isaiah that in a future time of blessing for the loyal remnant of His nominal people (Isaiah 65:8–10, 13–16), "the former troubles are forgotten and are hidden from my eyes" (verse 16). Then He gives the reason:

> "For behold, I create new heavens
>   and a new earth,
> and the former things shall not be remembered
>   or come into mind" (verse 17).

Among the new things in the re-created Earth, "the wolf and the lamb shall graze together; the lion shall eat straw like the ox" (verse 25). This reiterates the picture of peaceful tranquility in nature during the coming reign of the Messiah, which Isaiah 11:6, 9 introduced.

Isaiah 65 points ahead to the ultimate renewal of planet

Earth, which is also portrayed in Revelation 21:1–4. However, the era envisioned in Isaiah 65:20 includes death in Jerusalem:

> "No more shall there be in it
>   an infant who lives but a few days,
>   or an old man who does not fill out his days,
> for the young man shall die a hundred years old,
>   and the sinner a hundred years old shall be accursed."

The point is that God's people will be blessed with longevity (see also verse 22: "like the days of a tree"), although not yet immortality.

The scenario in Isaiah 65, when the people "shall build houses" (verse 21), is not yet the final restoration in Revelation 21 after the millennium, when God will have already built the New Jerusalem for His people (compare John 14:2) so that they will not need to construct houses for themselves. In this light, the expression "new heavens and a new earth" (Isaiah 65:17) and the peacefulness of the animals (verse 25) emphasize the radical extent of the transformation that the Lord desired for His faithful people in their Promised Land of Israel, and especially its capital of Jerusalem, before Christ's coming. However, like other predictions in classical prophecy (not including the apocalyptic prophecies in Daniel and Revelation), the prophecy of Isaiah 65 was conditional, depending on the response of God's people.

Although this prophecy could not be fulfilled in the present era, it will have a much greater fulfillment after Christ's second coming. At that time, God will literally re-create the heavens (the sky and atmosphere around the earth) and the earth, all creatures will be at peace, and there will be no more death.

Isaiah 66 continues to describe the future restoration of Jerusalem (verses 7–14) and reiterates the promise of "new heavens" and a "new earth" (verse 22), beginning with the concept that

God, as the Divine Creator, is big enough to accomplish such a vast transformation. He reminds His people,

> "Heaven is my throne,
>   and the earth is my footstool;
> what is the house that you would build for me,
>   and what is the place of my rest?
> All these things my hand has made,
>   and so all these things came to be" (verses 1, 2a;
>   compare 1 Kings 8:27).

Lest anyone think that God is so high, mighty, and transcendent that He is therefore inaccessible, Isaiah 66:2b adds the idea that He also "will look" to those who are humble and respect what He says (compare Isaiah 57:15). He is the "near" God (Deuteronomy 4:7), who pays attention to His people with favor and even answers before they call (Isaiah 65:24; see also Daniel 9:20–23). Other ancient Near Eastern peoples believed in high gods, who ruled the various domains of the cosmos, and lesser gods (including household and ancestral gods), to whom ordinary people could more easily appeal. But the Israelites needed only the one Lord, who fulfills all divine roles.

As noted earlier, the book of Isaiah presents its final appeal in the form of a radical contrast between the glorious destiny awaiting God's redeemed people (Isaiah 66:18–23) and the ignominious fate of those who persist in rebellion, whom He will annihilate (verse 24). The fact that God goes to the trouble of giving such warnings (for example, Revelation 14:9–11) shows that He is merciful, not wanting any to perish (see 2 Peter 3:9). He would not bother if He did not care. The warning is frightening, not because God is mean, but because the danger that He wants people to avoid is extreme.

As mentioned earlier in Isaiah, the future glory of God's loyal ones involves people from other nations coming to join them in honoring Him (Isaiah 66:18–21; see also Isaiah 2:2–4; 55:5; 60:3–16; 61:5, 6). All nations would gather to come and see God's glory (see Isaiah 66:18), and He would send "survivors," apparently of His Jewish remnant, to distant places in order to tell of His glory (verse 19). Christ's apostles fulfilled this prophecy, beginning in the book of Acts.

"And they shall bring all your brothers from all the nations as an offering to the LORD . . . to my holy mountain Jerusalem, says the LORD" (verse 20). Since "your brothers" would be Jews, this verse indicates that Gentiles who will have accepted God will bring dispersed Jews back to Him as a precious offering.

Isaiah 66:21 predicts a major change in the religious leadership: "And some of them also I will take for priests and for Levites, says the LORD." In this verse, "them" refers to the Gentiles, who are the primary subject of the previous verse. Previously, God had chosen the tribe of Levi for special service to Him (Exodus 32:26–29; Numbers 3; 4; 8), and from that tribe, He ordained Aaron and his descendants as His priests (Exodus 28; 29; Leviticus 8). Now the Lord announces that He will assign these roles to some people who are not even Israelites! This expands on the inclusion of foreigners as the Lord's servants (Isaiah 56:6) to signal the end of the exclusively Aaronic priesthood that was assisted by members of the Levite tribe.

Psalm 110:4 and Hebrews 5:6, 10 and 6:20 (see also Hebrews 7) explain the change of religious leadership. The Messiah, Christ, would establish a new kind of priesthood "after the order of Melchizedek" (Psalm 110:4), and Christ's followers would serve as "a royal priesthood" (1 Peter 2:9). But while there would be changes, the legacy (the descendants and the name) of God's chosen Jewish people would remain forever, as long "as the new heavens and the new earth" (Isaiah 66:22).

Life in the "new heavens and the new earth" will include regular, acceptable worship of God by His people, both Jewish and Gentile:

"From new moon to new moon,
  and from Sabbath to Sabbath,
all flesh shall come to worship before me,
declares the LORD" (Isaiah 66:23).

Here, at the end of Isaiah, we find positive correspondences to the negative elements at the beginning of the book, in which God's covenant lawsuit called on the "heavens" and "earth" as witnesses against His wayward people (Isaiah 1:2; compare Deuteronomy 30:19) and He rejected the hypocritical observance of "new moon and Sabbath" (Isaiah 1:13; see also verse 14).

The seventh-day Sabbath, which, by definition, is characterized by rest (*Sabbath* means "cessation"), is the unchangeable weekly "birthday" of planet Earth (Genesis 2:2, 3; Exodus 20:11). Thus, it makes sense that this day will continue to be sacred when God remakes our world into its ideal condition. As for new moons, Revelation 22:2 affirms the continuation of months in the new earth: the tree of life in the New Jerusalem will yield a different kind of fruit each month—no doubt eliciting monthly praise of God.

Seventh-day Sabbaths and new moons at the beginnings of months were special worship days for the ancient Israelites. At these times, the priests were to offer sacrifices on behalf of the whole community in addition to the morning and evening burnt offerings (Numbers 28:1–15). But in the ultimate new earth, worship on Sabbaths and new moons will not involve animal sacrifices because Christ's sacrifice fulfilled and therefore ended the need for the Israelite ritual system, including its observances during festivals (which encompassed ceremonial sabbaths), new moons, and Sabbaths (but not the basic Sabbath rest that commemorates Creation), which were "a shadow of the things to come" (Colossians 2:16, 17). So in the final new earth, there will be no need for the literal roles of "priests" and

"Levites" (Isaiah 66:21) to serve in such a ritual system as at the Lord's temple in Jerusalem (compare verse 20).

It appears that Isaiah's original audience was not ready to understand the major changes that would eventually come, also including the cessation of death (Isaiah 65:20). Therefore, God, through Isaiah, used language that was familiar in order to convey the conditional message of a limited but highly attractive future during the present era that would preview the unlimited glory of the new age to come.

Today we are close to that new era. Isaiah's vision of eternal happiness shines through the centuries to strengthen our trust and hope in God and our loyalty to Him. He offers us the world, literally, but a much better world. He does not force us to take His gift; the choice is ours. Where do you want to be?

---

1. For the biblical teaching of the final destruction of the wicked rather than an ever-burning torment in hell, see Edward W. Fudge, *The Fire That Consumes: A Biblical and Historical Study of the Doctrine of Final Punishment*, 3rd ed. (Eugene, OR: Cascade Books, 2011).